# The Northwest Indiana Directory of Local Scholarships: 2001–2002

Portage Public Library
2665 Irving Street
Portage, IN 46368

# The Northwest Indiana Directory of Local Scholarships: 2001–2002

## A Guide for Lake, LaPorte and Porter County Students

*Karen L. Williams*

Writers Club Press
San Jose  New York  Lincoln  Shanghai

The Northwest Indiana Directory of Local Scholarships: 2001–2002
A Guide for Lake, LaPorte and Porter County Students

All Rights Reserved © 2001 by Karen L. Williams

No part of this book may be reproduced or transmitted in any form or by any means, graphic, electronic, or mechanical, including photocopying, recording, taping, or by any information storage retrieval system, without the permission in writing from the publisher.

Writers Club Press
an imprint of iUniverse.com, Inc.

For information address:
iUniverse.com, Inc.
5220 S 16th, Ste. 200
Lincoln, NE 68512
www.iuniverse.com

ISBN: 0-595-18607-6

Printed in the United States of America

# CONTENTS

Foreward ..................................................................................... vii
Acknowledgements ..................................................................... ix
Introduction ................................................................................ xi
Guide to Locating Scholarships ..................................................... 1
    *When Do I Begin Looking For Scholarships?* .............................. 2
    *Maximize Your Child's Interest—Not Yours* .............................. 2
    *Summer Is Important, Too* ......................................................... 3
    *Where Do You Find These Scholarships?* .................................... 4
    *Applying for Financial Aid Assistance Through Colleges* ............ 6
    *State of Indiana Financial Assistance Programs* ......................... 6
Academic Scholarhips .................................................................. 9
Geographic Scholarships ............................................................ 25
Minority Scholarships ................................................................ 91
Need-Based Scholarhips ........................................................... 117
Organizational Scholarships ..................................................... 123
Returning Student Scholarhips ................................................. 143
School-Based Scholarhips ......................................................... 155
Vocational Scholarships ............................................................ 217
Links to Financial Aid and Scholarship Websites ...................... 255
Interested In Listing Your Scholarship? Fill Out The Form: ..... 257
References ................................................................................ 259

# FOREWARD

The information in this directory was compiled from private foundations, trusts, civic, business, post-secondary institutions, and religious organizations in the Northwest Indiana region. While every effort has been made to contact groups and organizations regarding their scholarship efforts, there may be many that are not listed. Many local chapters of civic or business organizations have no posted contact names, addresses or phone numbers. Because of this, many organizations were not contacted although they provide scholarships for students in their area. However, every attempt has been made to make sure that the information in this guide is accurate.

Local university and college scholarships were included if they were awarded to Northwest Indiana students. Some statewide/national scholarships from foundations or private trusts were included because the training for the vocation or the student population was so specific, that students at certain post-secondary institutions in Northwest Indiana would meet the criteria. *Generally, the scholarships listed are from Northwest Indiana region organizations that are given specifically to Northwest Indiana students.*

This directory is divided into the following alphabetized categories:

- *Academic*—awarded to students with a certain GPA, class rank or standardized test score.
- *Geographic*—awarded to students who reside in certain areas of a city or region.

- *Minority*—awarded to students who are in specified minority groups (ethnic, gender, religion, etc.).
- *Need-based*—awarded to students who show financial need.
- *Organizational*—awarded to students whose parents or the student is a member of a certain business, civic, or religious group.
- *Returning Student*—awarded to students who are graduate students or are currently enrolled in a post-secondary institution.
- *School-based*—awarded to students who attend or will attend a certain school.
- *Vocational*—awarded to student with a specified major or interest in a specific career.

**This directory *should not* be used in place of talking with high school or college financial aid advisors.**

I hope this guide will provide you with information to assist you and your student in your search for scholarships. While many of the scholarships won't get you through four years, they will give those finances a boost.

**Karen L. Williams**
Author
*The Northwest Indiana Directory of Local Scholarships: 2001—2002*
Klissell@yahoo.com

# ACKNOWLEDGEMENTS

Thanks to everyone who supported me while I "whined" about this project. Thanks goes to my daughter, Courtney, who was the inspiration for putting this work in book format, The Gary Educational Development Foundation, Maureen Crump-Hamblin and to Neal Modlinski for helping me with the technical areas.

# INTRODUCTION

Earning a college degree has become an integral part of the American Dream.

As students explore different career options, the ability to pay for a college education can often be **the** determining factor on what program of study and what college a student attends—or even if the student attends college at all. If the financial means are not available, affording a college education is an impossibility without the assistance of other financial aid resources. Government aid, college and university-sponsored efforts, and privately funded initiatives all provide variants of funding. But small local scholarships can also fill-in the gaps where others have left a need.

It is my hope that *The Northwest Indiana Directory of Local Scholarships: 2001—2002* will be used as a resource for all individuals living in Northwest Indiana who need additional financial aid to help pay for a college education. I encourage perspective and current students, as well as parents, to carefully peruse this comprehensive listing of financial aid resources.

Maureen R. Crump-Hamblin
Financial Aid Advisor
Ivy Tech State College
Valparaiso Campus
Valparaiso, IN

# Guide to Locating Scholarships

As the new millennium dawned, a survey by the American Council on Education showed that Americans still believe a college education is worth the money. However, 71 percent believe college is getting less affordable. Additionally, 83 percent of African Americans and 79 percent of Hispanics are more likely to think that college is not affordable. And while there are many books and counselors available, Americans still don't know where to get reliable information about financing a college education.

Every parent would love for his or her child to receive a full-tuition scholarship. But unless your child has an outstanding academic record or exceptional athletic ability, you may not get that full-tuition scholarship.

Several years ago I did some freelance work for a foundation that provided scholarships to graduating seniors. To my surprise, many of the scholarships did not require students to have extremely high grade point averages, extreme financial need or athletic ability. While most did not pay full-tuition (some were as low as $100), they did provide funds enough to buy books, pay room and board for a year, or supplemented other fees that were associated with attending a post-secondary institution.

Unlike the federal grants and loans, most scholarships do not require the parent to submit tax forms or apply through lengthy applications. Scholarships, which do not have to be paid back, do require the student to take an active role in applying. Either the student writes an essay, has a personal interview with a committee or supplies reference letters from teachers, employers or others in the community.

## When Do I Begin Looking For Scholarships?

*When* to begin looking for scholarships is more important than *where* to look for scholarships in the early stages. If you and your child wait until senior year to begin looking for funds, you have pretty much limited your success. While there are scholarships out there, there aren't enough to provide money to every child that wants or deserves one. I began looking at the different types of scholarships available when my daughter was in eighth grade. She is now a sophomore and will meet requirements for several scholarships when she is a senior.

Early on I realized that the successful candidates had built "resumes" over the course of years. Most scholarships require students to show a record of leadership, community involvement, or academic achievement over a period of time. The longer a child can show continued involvement in activities in the area the scholarship requires, the better his or her chances of receiving funds.

## Maximize Your *Child's* Interest—Not *Yours*

Your child may need to show a record of activity in the community or through school or church. It may be hard for some parents to allow their children to choose their own activities. And sometimes a little guidance is necessary, but it is important that the child has an interest in the activity. If the child likes the activity they will not only participate as a member, but also strive to take a leadership role in the organization. That does not mean they have to be president, although that certainly is a prestigious position, but they can participate on committees, in special events or any number of ways.

I developed a plan for my daughter when she was in the eighth grade. At the beginning of the school year we decide together which activities were the most interesting and offered the most challenge. The only requirement I had: one of the activities had to be academic in nature—foreign language, science, math, etc.

Once an activity was selected, she had to commit to participate either for a semester or the entire school year. By mandating the length of participation, she chose very wisely. Also, it gave her enough time in the organization to evaluate whether to continue the following year. My daughter enjoys academics and works diligently in those clubs and activities. She tried participating in an athletic activity, but at the end of the season she decided that it was not for her. However, she did stay throughout the entire season. If necessary she could add this to an application if asked.

It is also good for the child to show a record of service and community leadership. Consider organizations such as the scouts, 4-H club, church committees or civic groups that provide service projects at least once a year. And don't limit you child to local activities. If you can, try to involve them in regional, state and national activities as well.

## Summer Is Important, Too

Your child should also look for constructive activities for at least part of the summer. Some may choose to work while others may attend academic or athletic enrichment programs. They should attend a program where they can walk away from the experience with a broader view of themselves and the subject.

Summer is an excellent time to develop hobbies. Don't down play the hobbies your children have. My daughter loves to sew and craft. Those activities show creativity and tenacity. Put those activities and their outcome on the application under hobbies, skills and accomplishments.

Applying for scholarships is just like applying for a job. You have to show a record of achievement and skills that fit the position to get the job. So it is with scholarships. Build a solid resume.

# Where Do You Find These Scholarships?

Your child's school is a good resource for scholarships. Guidance counselors are usually the first point of contact for most organizations. Most schools post information on an information board. But it is difficult to let every child know what scholarships are available. So, it is really up to the student to check for information on his own. Along with scanning the local newspaper under organization news, here are a few places to check:

### Businesses and Corporations

Start with businesses and corporations in your town or in your state. Their requirements may be less strenuous than some of the national companies. Call the public relations department for information. They will be able to lead you in the right direction. After, you have explored your options with the locals, begin to look for scholarships from the national companies like Ford Motor Company and Coca-Cola to name a few. An internet search may provide information about others.

### Private Scholarships/Foundations

Private scholarships are provided by trust funds, memorial funds, foundations or individuals. These scholarships may have very specific requirements such as residence, school, interests or hobbies.

### Clubs and Groups in Your Community

Even if your aren't a member of any local civic groups and organizations like the Optimist Club or Kiwanis, your child may still be eligible based on his involvement in the community.

## College-based Scholarships

College-based scholarships are provided by the local/regional college to students who meet certain academic requirements. Most rely on SAT or ACT scores, high school ranking, choice of major or residence.

## Professional Societies and Associations

Professional societies and associations offer scholarships to encourage students to choose majors in a certain field. Check with medical, engineering or teaching organizations. Use the internet to find professional societies in the field that your child will be majoring. They may possibly be offering money to students.

## Religious Organizations

Churches and other places of worship often sponsor scholarships. Check with worship-oriented service groups. You may not have to be a member. Some will provide scholarships to students who plan to major in the particular religion or belief.

## Minority Organizations

To provide for increased minority diversity, organizations such as the United Negro College Fund, many sororities or fraternities, and some civic organizations use race, ethnicity, religion, or gender as eligibility requirements for their scholarships.

## Your Job

Check with your union and place of employment. Some of these scholarships are based on length of membership or employment; however, they are an excellent starting point.

## Applying for Financial Aid Assistance Through Colleges

Most colleges, universities and technical schools provide advice to students who may need financial assistance in order to attend school. Applications for financial assistance are processed and financial need is calculated based on the assumption that the primary responsibility for paying college costs rests with the family. Priority for all services is given to students and families submitting all required forms by the deadline set by the institution.

Also, each institution may have other eligibility requirements that must be met. Those requirements may include:

- Signed copy of parent or student's federal income tax return and schedules or other forms from the IRS.

- Copies of all W-2 forms, pension, IRA, dividend, interest statements, and state tax forms;

- And records of untaxed income (AFDC)

## State of Indiana Financial Assistance Programs

Full-time undergraduate students who demonstrate financial need and who are Indiana residents may receive a tuition and mandatory fee remission award through the State of Indiana for the first four years of college. Because the award is subsidized by the Federal government through State Student Incentive Grant funding, students may be required to meet federal eligibility requirements. The school will require you to complete a Free Application for Federal Student Aid (FAFSA) that must be submitted to the Federal Processor by March 1. Students must specify the name of the institution to receive a copy of the analysis. SSACI award notifications are mailed in June by the SSACI, ISTA Center, 150 W. Market Street, Indianapolis, IN 46204-1088, phone (317) 232-2350.

# ACADEMIC SCHOLARHIPS

| | |
|---|---|
| Type | Academic |
| Major | All |
| Scholarship Name | Calumet College of St. Joseph Academic Scholarship |
| City | Whiting |
| Organization | Calumet College of St. Joseph |
| Amount | Up to 50% of tuition |
| Annual/One-Time | Annual |
| Requirements | For a current academic-year high school graduate with a GPA of 3.50 or higher. Recipients must register for 12 or more credit hours per semester. Renewable if a 3.00 or higher GPA is maintained at Calumet College of St. Joseph. |
| Deadline | See Financial Aid Director |
| Contact Name | Financial Aid Director |
| Address | Calumet College of St. Joseph 2400 New York Ave |
| State | IN |
| Zip Code | 46394 |
| Phone | 219-473-7770 |
| Fax | |
| E-mail | finaid@ccsj.edu |
| Notes | All students are encouraged to complete a free application for Federal Student Aid (FAFSA). Deadline is March 1. |

| | |
|---|---|
| Type | Academic |
| Major | All |
| Scholarship Name | Calumet College of St. Joseph Scholarship |
| City | Whiting |
| Organization | Calumet College of St. Joseph |
| Amount | $2,000—$8,000 during four years. |
| Annual/One-Time | Annual |
| Requirements | The student must be a graduate of a Lake or Porter county high school. The student must enroll at Calumet College of St. Joseph in September for a minimum of 12 credit hours, complete all federal and state financial aid applications, have a 2.5 or higher GPA on a 4.0 scale, SAT score of 850 or 18 on the ACT and rank in the top 25 percent of their class. In order to receive the scholarship annually, the student must maintain a 3.0 average. |
| Deadline | June 15 |
| Contact Name | High School Guidance Counselor or |
| Address | Calumet College of St. Joseph 2400 New York Ave |
| State | IN |
| Zip Code | 46394 |
| Phone | 219-473-7770 |
| Fax | |
| E-mail | finaid@ccsj.edu |

**Notes**

All students are encouraged to complete a free application for Federal Student Aid (FAFSA). Deadline is March 1.

| | |
|---|---|
| Type | Academic |
| Major | All |
| Scholarship Name | Chancellor's Council Scholarship |
| City | Hammond |
| Organization | Purdue University Calumet |
| Amount | Contact Director of Financial Aid |
| Annual/One-Time | One Time |
| Requirements | The student must be in the top 10% of his or her graduating class and have a combined SAT of 1200. The student must also have a GPA of 3.5 or above. |
| Deadline | March 1 |
| Contact Name | Office of Financial Aid |
| Address | Purdue University Calumet 2200 169th Street |
| State | IN |
| Zip Code | 46323-2094 |
| Phone | 219-989-2301 |
| Fax | 219-989-2772 |
| E-mail | finaid@calumet.purdue.edu |
| Notes | Student should also complete the Purdue Calumet Merit Scholarship Application. |

| | |
|---|---|
| Type | Academic |
| Major | All |
| Scholarship Name | Chancellor's Salutatorian Scholarship |
| City | Gary |
| Organization | Indiana University Northwest |
| Amount | Full Academic Scholarship |
| Annual/One-Time | Annual |
| Requirements | These scholarships are available to each salutatorian from an accredited high school in Northwest Indiana who meet established admission requirements and enrolls full-time. The scholarships are renewable annually providing established academic criteria are satisfied. |
| Deadline | See Financial Aid Director |
| Contact Name | Director of Financial Aid |
| Address | Indiana University Northwest 3400 Broadway |
| State | IN |
| Zip Code | 46408 |
| Phone | 219-980-6777 |
| Fax | |
| E-mail | Klantz@iunhaw1.iun.indiana.edu |
| Notes | All students are encouraged to complete a free application for Federal Student Aid (FAFSA). Deadline is March 1. |

| | |
|---|---|
| Type | Academic |
| Major | All |
| Scholarship Name | Chancellor's Valedictorian Scholarship |
| City | Gary |
| Organization | Indiana University Northwest |
| Amount | Full Academic Scholarship |
| Annual/One-Time | Annual |
| Requirements | These scholarships are available to each valedictorian from an accredited high school in Northwest Indiana who meet established admission requirements and enrolls full-time. The scholarship is renewable annually providing established academic criteria are satisfied. |
| Deadline | See Financial Aid Director |
| Contact Name | Director of Financial Aid |
| Address | Indiana University Northwest 3400 Broadway |
| State | IN |
| Zip Code | 46408 |
| Phone | 219-980-6777 |
| Fax | |
| E-mail | Klantz@iunhaw1.iun.indiana.edu |
| Notes | All students are encouraged to complete a free application for Federal Student Aid (FAFSA). Deadline is March 1. |

| | |
|---|---|
| Type | Academic |
| Major | All |
| Scholarship Name | **Emerging Scholars Grant** |
| City | Whiting |
| Organization | Calumet College of St. Joseph |
| Amount | See Financial Aid Director |
| Annual/One-Time | One Time |
| Requirements | For current academic-year high school graduates with a 2.50 or higher GPA, composite ACT score of 18 or higher, combined SAT score of 850 or higher and recipients must register for 12 or more credit hours per semester. |
| Deadline | See Financial Aid Director |
| Contact Name | Director of Financial Aid |
| Address | Calumet College of St. Joseph 2400 New York Ave. |
| State | IN |
| Zip Code | 46394 |
| Phone | 219-473-7770 |
| Fax | |
| E-mail | finaid@cccsj.edu |
| Notes | All students are encouraged to complete a free application for Federal Student Aid (FAFSA). Deadline is March 1. |

| | |
|---|---|
| Type | Academic |
| Major | All |
| Scholarship Name | Harris, J. Glenn and Gladys Scholarship |
| City | Gary |
| Organization | Indiana University Northwest |
| Amount | Full tuition |
| Annual/One-Time | One Time |
| Requirements | The scholarship is open to junior and seniors at IUN who excel academically and have a financial need. |
| Deadline | See Financial Aid Director |
| Contact Name | Director of Financial Aid |
| Address | Indiana University Northwest 3400 Broadway |
| State | IN |
| Zip Code | 46408 |
| Phone | 219-980-6777 |
| Fax | |
| E-mail | Klantz@iunhaw1.iun.indiana.edu |
| Notes | All students are encouraged to complete a free application for Federal Student Aid (FAFSA). Deadline is March 1. |

| | |
|---|---|
| Type | Academic |
| Major | All |
| Scholarship Name | Indiana University Northwest Academic Scholarships for |
| City | Gary |
| Organization | Indiana University Northwest |
| Amount | Up to tuition, fees and books |
| Annual/One-Time | One Time |
| Requirements | Academic merit. |
| Deadline | April |
| Contact Name | Financial Aid Director |
| Address | IU Northwest<br>3400 Broadway |
| State | IN |
| Zip Code | 46408 |
| Phone | 219-980-6777 |
| Fax | |
| E-mail | Klantz@iunhaw1.iun.indiana.edu |
| Notes | All students are encouraged to complete a free application for Federal Student Aid (FAFSA). Deadline is March 1. |

| | |
|---|---|
| Type | Academic |
| Major | All |
| Scholarship Name | **Lutheran's President's Award** |
| City | Valparaiso |
| Organization | Valparaiso University |
| Amount | $1000—$2000 |
| Annual/One-Time | Annual |
| Requirements | The award is given to an entering Freshman based on academic leadership and academic achievement and is renewable with a 2.0 GPA. The student must be an entering Freshman. Awards based on academic leadership and academic achievement |
| Deadline | March 1 |
| Contact Name | Director of Financial Aid |
| Address | Valparaiso University Kretzmann Hall |
| State | IN |
| Zip Code | 46383 |
| Phone | 219-464-5015 or |
| Fax | |
| E-mail | finaid@valpo.edu |
| Notes | All students are encouraged to complete a free application for Federal Student Aid (FAFSA). Deadline is March 1. |

| | |
|---|---|
| Type | Academic |
| Major | All |
| Scholarship Name | **Purdue Club of Lake County Scholarship** |
| City | Hammond |
| Organization | Purdue Club of Lake County |
| Amount | Open |
| Annual/One-Time | One Time |
| Requirements | Academic merit and Lake or Porter County resident. |
| Deadline | April |
| Contact Name | Purdue Club of Lake County |
| Address | Purdue University Calumet 2200 169th Street |
| State | IN |
| Zip Code | 46323 |
| Phone | 219-989-2301 |
| Fax | 219-989-2771 |
| E-mail | |
| Notes | |

| | |
|---|---|
| Type | Academic |
| Major | All |
| Scholarship Name | Special Academic Scholars Scholarship |
| City | Gary |
| Organization | Indiana University Northwest |
| Amount | Full tuition |
| Annual/One-Time | Annual |
| Requirements | These full-tuition scholarships are open to freshmen in the top 10 percent of their graduating class with superior SAT scores. They are renewable yearly if academic criteria are maintained. Selections are made by the admissions office. |
| Deadline | Contact Financial Aid |
| Contact Name | Director of Financial Aid |
| Address | Indiana University Northwest 3400 Broadway |
| State | IN |
| Zip Code | 46408 |
| Phone | 219-980-6777 |
| Fax | |
| E-mail | Klantz@iunhaw1.iun.indiana.edu |
| Notes | All students are encouraged to complete a free application for Federal Student Aid (FAFSA). Deadline is March 1. |

| | |
|---|---|
| Type | Academic |
| Major | Chemistry |
| Scholarship Name | Amoco Scholarship |
| City | Gary |
| Organization | Indiana University Northwest |
| Amount | See Financial Aid Director |
| Annual/One-Time | One Time |
| Requirements | The scholarship is awarded to students who hold junior standing with a GPA of 3.0. Preference is given to students who are residents of Lake or Porter counties. |
| Deadline | See Financial Aid Director |
| Contact Name | Director of Financial Aid |
| Address | Indiana University Northwest 3400 Broadway |
| State | IN |
| Zip Code | 46404 |
| Phone | 219-980-6777 |
| Fax | |
| E-mail | Klantz@iunhaw1.iun.indiana.edu |
| Notes | All students are encouraged to complete a free application for Federal Student Aid (FAFSA). Deadline is March 1. |

| | |
|---|---|
| Type | Academic |
| Major | Political Science |
| Scholarship Name | Ryan Scholarship |
| City | Gary |
| Organization | Indiana University Northwest |
| Amount | $500 |
| Annual/One-Time | One Time |
| Requirements | The scholarship is awarded annually to two academically meritorious undergraduates. |
| Deadline | Contact Financial Aid Director |
| Contact Name | Director of Financial Aid |
| Address | Indiana University Northwest 3400 Broadway |
| State | IN |
| Zip Code | 46408 |
| Phone | 219-980-6777 |
| Fax | |
| E-mail | Klantz@iunhaw1.iun.indiana.edu |
| Notes | All students are encouraged to complete a free application for Federal Student Aid (FAFSA). Deadline is March 1. |

# Geographic Scholarships

| | |
|---|---|
| Type | Geographic |
| Major | All |
| Scholarship Name | Academic Promise |
| City | Gary |
| Organization | Gary Educational Development Foundation |
| Amount | $800 |
| Annual/One-Time | One Time |
| Requirements | The graduating senior must be a student at a Gary high school. Priority is given to candidates entering a four-year college or university, have high academic accomplishments and a need for financial assistance. Students must maintain a GPA of 2.0 during the duration of the scholarship. |
| Deadline | April |
| Contact Name | High School Guidance Counselor or |
| Address | The Gary Educational Development Foundation 3757 W. 21st Ave. |
| State | IN |
| Zip Code | 46404 |
| Phone | 219 977-2192 |
| Fax | 219-977-6258 |
| E-mail | |
| Notes | |

| | |
|---|---|
| Type | Geographic |
| Major | All |
| Scholarship Name | Barney's Hub Bootery Scholarship IV |
| City | Crown Point |
| Organization | Crown Point Community Foundation, Inc. |
| Amount | $1000 |
| Annual/One-Time | Annual |
| Requirements | For Crown Point residents pursuing a college degree or vocational education. |
| Deadline | April 15 |
| Contact Name | Crown Point Community Foundation, Inc. |
| Address | P.O. Box 522 |
| State | IN |
| Zip Code | 46308-0522 |
| Phone | 219-662-7252 |
| Fax | 219-662-9493 |
| E-mail | cpcf@ursip.com |
| Notes | |

| | |
|---|---|
| **Type** | Geographic |
| **Major** | All |
| **Scholarship Name** | Battle, Haron J. Dr. |
| **City** | Gary |
| **Organization** | Gary Educational Development Foundation |
| **Amount** | $500 |
| **Annual/One-Time** | One Time |
| **Requirements** | The graduating senior must be a student at a Gary high school. The student must have a sound career goal in mind. |
| **Deadline** | April |
| **Contact Name** | High School Guidance Counselor or |
| **Address** | Gary Educational Development Foundation<br>3757 W. 21st. Ave. |
| **State** | IN |
| **Zip Code** | 46404 |
| **Phone** | 219-977-2192 |
| **Fax** | 219-977-6258 |
| **E-mail** | |
| **Notes** | |

| | |
|---|---|
| Type | Geographic |
| Major | All |
| Scholarship Name | Battle, Ruth Scholarship |
| City | Gary |
| Organization | Gary Educational Development Foundation |
| Amount | $1000 |
| Annual/One-Time | One Time |
| Requirements | One student selected buy the GEDF. Student must have a sound career goal in mind. Each Gary high school will submit one applicant. |
| Deadline | April |
| Contact Name | High School Guidance Counselor or |
| Address | The Gary Educational Development Foundation 3757 W. 21st Ave. |
| State | IN |
| Zip Code | 46404 |
| Phone | 219 977-2192 |
| Fax | 219-977-6258 |
| E-mail | |
| Notes | |

| | |
|---|---|
| Type | Geographic |
| Major | All |
| Scholarship Name | Birdzell, Dr. John P. and Helen M. Scholarship |
| City | Crown Point |
| Organization | Crown Point Community Foundation |
| Amount | $1000 |
| Annual/One-Time | One Time |
| Requirements | Residents of Crown Point. |
| Deadline | March 1 |
| Contact Name | Crown Point Community Foundation |
| Address | P.O. Box 522 |
| State | IN |
| Zip Code | 46308-522 |
| Phone | 219-662-7252 |
| Fax | 219-662-9493 |
| E-mail | cpcf@ursip.com |
| Notes | |

| | |
|---|---|
| Type | Geographic |
| Major | All |
| Scholarship Name | Butcher, Marguerite Lopez Scholarship |
| City | Gary |
| Organization | Gary Educational Development Foundation |
| Amount | $800 |
| Annual/One-Time | Annual |
| Requirements | The graduating senior must be a student at a Gary high school and possess a GPA commensurate with the requirements of the institution of choice, demonstrated financial need and have an educational plan. |
| Deadline | April |
| Contact Name | High School Guidance Counselor or |
| Address | The Gary Educational Development Foundation<br>3757 W. 21st. Ave. |
| State | IN |
| Zip Code | 46404 |
| Phone | 219 977-2192 |
| Fax | 219-977-6258 |
| E-mail | |
| Notes | |

| | |
|---|---|
| Type | Geographic |
| Major | All |
| Scholarship Name | **Community Leader Awards** |
| City | Bentonville |
| Organization | Wal-Mart Foundation |
| Amount | $1000 |
| Annual/One-Time | One Time |
| Requirements | Academic merit, leadership and financial need for a student in a Wal-Mart service area. |
| Deadline | January |
| Contact Name | Wal-Mart Foundation |
| Address | Sam Walton Community Scholarship Program 702 S.N. 8th Street |
| State | AR |
| Zip Code | 72716-8071 |
| Phone | |
| Fax | |
| E-mail | |
| Notes | Contact your local Wal-Mart for further details. |

| | |
|---|---|
| Type | Geographic |
| Major | All |
| Scholarship Name | Davis, Herschel B. Scholarship |
| City | Gary |
| Organization | Gary Educational Development Foundation |
| Amount | $800 |
| Annual/One-Time | One Time |
| Requirements | The graduating senior must be a student at a Gary high school pursuing a post-secondary education. |
| Deadline | April |
| Contact Name | High School Guidance Counselor or |
| Address | The Gary Educational Development Foundation 3757 W. 21st. Ave. |
| State | IN |
| Zip Code | 46404 |
| Phone | 219-977-2192 |
| Fax | 219-977-6258 |
| E-mail | |
| Notes | |

| | |
|---|---|
| Type | Geographic |
| Major | All |
| Scholarship Name | Dye, Jim and Betty Scholarship |
| City | Gary |
| Organization | Indiana University Northwest |
| Amount | See Financial Aid Director |
| Annual/One-Time | Annual |
| Requirements | This scholarship is awarded to an incoming freshman student who is a resident of Griffith. The award may be renewable for 3 years. |
| Deadline | See Financial Aid Director |
| Contact Name | Director of Financial Aid |
| Address | Indiana University Northwest 3400 Broadway |
| State | IN |
| Zip Code | 46408 |
| Phone | 219-980-6777 |
| Fax | |
| E-mail | Klantz@iunhaw1.iun.indiana.edu |
| Notes | All students are encouraged to complete a free application for Federal Student Aid (FAFSA). Deadline is March 1. |

| | |
|---|---|
| Type | Geographic |
| Major | All |
| Scholarship Name | Gary Housing Authority Commissioners' Four Year Scholarship |
| City | Gary |
| Organization | Gary Educational Development Foundation |
| Amount | $3200 |
| Annual/One-Time | One Time |
| Requirements | The graduating senior must be a resident in the Gary Housing Authority conventional apartment units. The scholarship is offered every four years. Students must have a good record of positive high school experiences and achievements, have demonstrated positive qualities of leadership and citizenship. |
| Deadline | April |
| Contact Name | High School Guidance Counselor or |
| Address | The Gary Educational Development Foundation 3757 W. 21st Ave. |
| State | IN |
| Zip Code | 46404 |
| Phone | 219-977-2192 |
| Fax | 219-977-6258 |
| E-mail | |
| Notes | |

| | |
|---|---|
| Type | Geographic |
| Major | All |
| Scholarship Name | **Gary Housing Authority Public Housing Authority Resident** |
| City | Gary |
| Organization | Gary Educational Development Foundation |
| Amount | $800 |
| Annual/One-Time | One Time |
| Requirements | The graduating senior must be a resident of the Gary Housing Authority conventional apartment units. The student must have a record of positive high school experiences and citizenship, demonstrated qualities of leadership, have an appropriate postsecondary plan including choice of institution and studies. |
| Deadline | April |
| Contact Name | High School Guidance Counselor or |
| Address | The Gary Educational Development Foundation 3757 W. 21st Ave. |
| State | IN |
| Zip Code | 46404 |
| Phone | 219-977-2192 |
| Fax | 219-977-6258 |
| E-mail | |
| Notes | |

| | |
|---|---|
| Type | Geographic |
| Major | All |
| Scholarship Name | Gary Teacher's Union Local #4/Charles Smith |
| City | Gary |
| Organization | Gary Educational Development Foundation |
| Amount | $700 |
| Annual/One-Time | One Time |
| Requirements | The graduating senior must be a student at a Gary high school. |
| Deadline | April |
| Contact Name | High School Guidance Counselor or |
| Address | The Gary Educational Development Foundation 3757 W. 21st Ave. |
| State | IN |
| Zip Code | 46404 |
| Phone | 219-977-2192 |
| Fax | 219-977-6258 |
| E-mail | |
| Notes | |

| | |
|---|---|
| Type | Geographic |
| Major | All |
| Scholarship Name | Gary's 75th Anniversary |
| City | Gary |
| Organization | Gary Educational Development Foundation |
| Amount | $1000 |
| Annual/One-Time | One Time |
| Requirements | The graduating senior must be a student at a Gary high school. Student must have a GPA of 2.0 or better and have a sound career goal. |
| Deadline | April |
| Contact Name | High School Guidance Counselor or |
| Address | The Gary Educational Development Foundation 3757 W. 21st. Ave. |
| State | IN |
| Zip Code | 46404 |
| Phone | 219-977-2192 |
| Fax | 219-977-6258 |
| E-mail | |
| Notes | |

| | |
|---|---|
| Type | Geographic |
| Major | All |
| Scholarship Name | **Griffith Chamber of Commerce** |
| City | Griffith |
| Organization | Griffith Chamber of Commerce |
| Amount | $500 |
| Annual/One-Time | One Time |
| Requirements | Griffith residents. |
| Deadline | April 9 |
| Contact Name | Griffith Chamber of Commerce |
| Address | 201 S. Broad Street |
| | P.O. Box 204 |
| State | IN |
| Zip Code | 46319 |
| Phone | 219-924-2155 |
| Fax | 219-838-2661 |
| E-mail | GCC@conceptvision.com |
| Notes | |

| | |
|---|---|
| Type | Geographic |
| Major | All |
| Scholarship Name | Hammond Centennial Scholarship |
| City | Hammond |
| Organization | Purdue University Calumet |
| Amount | Contact Financial Aid Office |
| Annual/One-Time | One Time |
| Requirements | The student must be an undergraduate with a GPA of 3.0. |
| Deadline | March 1 |
| Contact Name | Office of Financial Aid |
| Address | Purdue University Calumet 2200 169th Street |
| State | IN |
| Zip Code | 46323-2094 |
| Phone | 219-989-2301 |
| Fax | 219-989-2771 |
| E-mail | finaid@calumet.purdue.edu |
| Notes | All students are encouraged to complete a free application for Federal Student Aid (FAFSA) and Merit Scholarship Application. |

| | |
|---|---|
| Type | Geographic |
| Major | All |
| Scholarship Name | Hammond Optimist Scholarship |
| City | Hammond |
| Organization | Purdue University Calumet |
| Amount | Contact Director of Financial Aid |
| Annual/One-Time | One Time |
| Requirements | Student must resident in Hammond. |
| Deadline | March 1 |
| Contact Name | Office of Financial Aid |
| Address | Purdue University Calumet 2200 169th Street |
| State | IN |
| Zip Code | 46323-2094 |
| Phone | 219-989-2301 |
| Fax | 219-989-2771 |
| E-mail | finaid@calumet.purdue.edu |
| Notes | All students are encouraged to complete a free application for Federal Student Aid (FAFSA) and the Merit Scholarship form. |

*Karen L. Williams*

| | |
|---|---|
| Type | Geographic |
| Major | All |
| Scholarship Name | Harrison, Edgar A Sr./Alpha Chi Chapter-Omega Psi Phi |
| City | Gary |
| Organization | Gary Educational Development Foundation |
| Amount | $1000 |
| Annual/One-Time | One Time |
| Requirements | Award given to a Gary high school graduating senior. Student must be pursuing a worthy career development plan in an accredited post-secondary educational institution. |
| Deadline | April |
| Contact Name | High School Guidance Counselor or |
| Address | Gary Educational Development Foundation<br>3757 W. 21st. Ave. |
| State | IN |
| Zip Code | 46404 |
| Phone | 219-977-2192 |
| Fax | 219-977-6258 |
| E-mail | |
| Notes | |

| | |
|---|---|
| Major | Geographic All |
| Scholarship Name | Helmchen, Christel R./GAP Scholarship |
| City | Valparaiso |
| Organization | Christel R. Helmchen/GAP Scholarship |
| Amount | $1000 |
| Annual/One-Time | One Time |
| Requirements | Three scholarships awarded each to a senior from Chesterton, Valparaiso and Michigan City. |
| Deadline | Contact Fund |
| Contact Name | Christel R. Helmchen/GAP Scholarship Fund |
| Address | 839 N. 400 E |
| State | IN |
| Zip Code | 46383 |
| Phone | |
| Fax | |
| E-mail | |
| Notes | |

| | |
|---|---|
| **Type** | **Geographic** |
| **Major** | **All** |
| **Scholarship Name** | **Highland Dollars for Scholars** |
| **City** | Highland |
| **Organization** | Highland School System |
| **Amount** | $3000 |
| **Annual/One-Time** | One Time |
| **Requirements** | Highland Residents. |
| **Deadline** | April 16 |
| **Contact Name** | Dollars For Scholars |
| **Address** | Highland School System |
| | 9145 Kennedy Ave. |
| **State** | IN |
| **Zip Code** | 46322 |
| **Phone** | |
| **Fax** | |
| **E-mail** | |
| **Notes** | |

| | |
|---|---|
| Type | Geographic |
| Major | All |
| Scholarship Name | Howard, John Lee Scholarship |
| City | Gary |
| Organization | Gary Educational Development Foundation |
| Amount | $800 |
| Annual/One-Time | One Time |
| Requirements | The graduating senior must be a student at a Gary high school. Student must attend a post-secondary institution in preparation for a sound career goal. A 200-word essay is required to be submitted with the application. |
| Deadline | April |
| Contact Name | High School Guidance Counselor or |
| Address | The Gary Educational Development Foundation 3757 W. 21st. Ave. |
| State | IN |
| Zip Code | 46404 |
| Phone | 219-977-2192 |
| Fax | 219-977-6258 |
| E-mail | |
| Notes | Funded by Mayor Thomas V. Barnes' New Direction Committee |

| | |
|---|---|
| Type | Geographic |
| Major | All |
| Scholarship Name | James, Julius Reverend Scholarship |
| City | Gary |
| Organization | Gary Educational Development Foundation |
| Amount | $1000 |
| Annual/One-Time | One Time |
| Requirements | The graduating senior must be a student at a Gary high school and possess a GPA of 2.5 or better and have an educational plan. |
| Deadline | April |
| Contact Name | High School Guidance Counselor or |
| Address | Gary Educational Development Foundation 3757 W. 21st. Ave. |
| State | IN |
| Zip Code | 46404 |
| Phone | 219-977-2192 |
| Fax | 219-977-6258 |
| E-mail | |
| Notes | |

| | |
|---|---|
| Type | Geographic |
| Major | All |
| Scholarship Name | Kiwanis/Eskilson/Tuchek/Tyler Scholarship |
| City | Gary |
| Organization | Gary Educational Development Foundation |
| Amount | $800 |
| Annual/One-Time | One Time |
| Requirements | The graduating senior must be a student at a Gary high school and have a positive school experience, demonstrate high positive qualities of character and service, and displays personal qualities observed directly or through references and have a reasonable conception of career goals. |
| Deadline | April |
| Contact Name | High School Guidance Counselor or |
| Address | The Gary Educational Development Foundation 3757 W. 21st Ave. |
| State | IN |
| Zip Code | 46404 |
| Phone | 219-977-2192 |
| Fax | 219-977-6258 |
| E-mail | |
| Notes | |

*Karen L. Williams*

| | |
|---|---|
| Type | Geographic |
| Major | All |
| Scholarship Name | Lilly Endowment Community Scholarship |
| City | Michigan City |
| Organization | Unity Foundation of LaPorte County, Inc. |
| Amount | Full-tuition for four years |
| Annual/One-Time | One Time |
| Requirements | Must plan to attend an Indiana public or private college accredited by the North Central Association of Colleges and working toward a degree. Students must have excellent academic and community service record. Demonstrated leadership, commitment and employment history. Two students will be selected. Must be a resident of LaPorte. |
| Deadline | February |
| Contact Name | Unity Foundation of LaPorte County, Inc. |
| Address | P.O. Box 527 |
| State | IN |
| Zip Code | 46361 |
| Phone | 219-879-0327 |
| Fax | |
| E-mail | |
| Notes | |

| | |
|---|---|
| **Major** | |
| | **Geographic** |
| | **All** |
| **Scholarship Name** | **Lilly Endowment Community Scholarship Program** |
| **City** | Valparaiso |
| **Organization** | Porter County Community Scholarship |
| **Amount** | Full tuition |
| **Annual/One-Time** | One Time |
| **Requirements** | Student must be a resident of Porter County, a graduate of an accredited Indiana High School and must be accepted for a full-time, four-year baccalaureate course of study. Available also for students who graduated but never attended college. |
| **Deadline** | April |
| **Contact Name** | High School Guidance Counselor or |
| **Address** | Porter County Community Foundation |
| **State** | IN |
| **Zip Code** | 46384 |
| **Phone** | 219-465-0294 |
| **Fax** | |
| **E-mail** | pccf@niia.net |
| **Notes** | |

| | |
|---|---|
| Type | Geographic |
| Major | All |
| Scholarship Name | Marshall, Thurgood Justice Scholarship |
| City | Gary |
| Organization | Gary Educational Development Foundation |
| Amount | $1000 |
| Annual/One-Time | One Time |
| Requirements | The graduating senior must be a student at a Gary high school and have a reasonable conception of goals, display exemplary qualities of leadership and appropriate post-secondary education plan including the college and program of studies. |
| Deadline | April |
| Contact Name | High School Guidance Counselor or |
| Address | The Gary Educational Development Foundation 3757 W. 21st Ave. |
| State | IN |
| Zip Code | 46404 |
| Phone | 219-977-2192 |
| Fax | 219-977-6258 |
| E-mail | |
| Notes | |

| | |
|---|---|
| Type | Geographic |
| Major | All |
| Scholarship Name | Maywood Civic Club |
| City | Hammond |
| Organization | Purdue University Calumet |
| Amount | Contact Financial Aid Office |
| Annual/One-Time | One Time |
| Requirements | For Hammond residents with a 3.0 GPA and will carry 12 hours of credits. |
| Deadline | March 1 |
| Contact Name | Office of Financial Aid |
| Address | Purdue University Calumet 2200 169th Street |
| State | IN |
| Zip Code | 46323-2094 |
| Phone | 219-989-2301 |
| Fax | 219-989-2771 |
| E-mail | finaid@calumet.purdue.edu |
| Notes | Merit Scholarship application required. |

| | |
|---|---|
| Type | Geographic |
| Major | All |
| Scholarship Name | Michigan City Scholarship Foundation |
| City | Michigan City |
| Organization | Michigan City Scholarship Foundation |
| Amount | $1000 average |
| Annual/One-Time | Annual |
| Requirements | Michigan City or Marquette High students. Awards based on financial need, scholastic record, motivation/ability to succeed. All awards begin as a loan with no interest. Upon proof of graduation, half of the loan is forgiven. The balance to be repaid in three years. |
| Deadline | June |
| Contact Name | Sharon Ginther |
| Address | Michigan City Area Schools Administration Bldg. 408 S. Carroll |
| State | IN |
| Zip Code | 46360 |
| Phone | 219-873-2000 |
| Fax | |
| E-mail | |
| Notes | Also available to graduate students. |

| | |
|---|---|
| Type | Geographic |
| Major | All |
| Scholarship Name | National City Bank Scholarship |
| City | Hammond |
| Organization | Purdue University Calumet |
| Amount | Contact Office of Financial Aid |
| Annual/One-Time | One Time |
| Requirements | For freshmen students who live in Munster, Merrillville, Schererville and East Chicago with a 2.5 GPA and are enrolled in 12 hours. |
| Deadline | March 1 |
| Contact Name | Office of Financial Aid |
| Address | Purdue University Calumet<br>2200 169th Street |
| State | IN |
| Zip Code | 46323-2094 |
| Phone | 219-989-2307 |
| Fax | 219-989-2771 |
| E-mail | finaid@calumet.purdue.edu |
| Notes | Students must complete both a Merit Scholarship application and National City Bank Scholarship application. |

| | |
|---|---|
| **Type** | Geographic |
| **Major** | All |
| **Scholarship Name** | Optimist Club of Merrillville Annual Scholarship Award |
| **City** | Merrillville |
| **Organization** | Optimist Club of Merrillville |
| **Amount** | Open |
| **Annual/One-Time** | One Time |
| **Requirements** | College bound students from Merrillville. |
| **Deadline** | May |
| **Contact Name** | Keith Lennon |
| **Address** | 8705 Merrillville Rd. |
| **State** | IN |
| **Zip Code** | 46410-7045 |
| **Phone** | 219-756-0911 |
| **Fax** | |
| **E-mail** | |
| **Notes** | |

| | |
|---|---|
| Type | Geographic |
| Major | All |
| Scholarship Name | **Schererville Civic Funds** |
| City | Schererville |
| Organization | Town of Schererville |
| Amount | $1000 |
| Annual/One-Time | One Time |
| Requirements | Schererville residents with a minimum of a 2.0 GPA. |
| Deadline | April |
| Contact Name | Dick Crane |
| Address | City Manager, Town of Schererville 833 W. Lincoln Hwy |
| State | IN |
| Zip Code | 46375 |
| Phone | 219-322-2211 |
| Fax | |
| E-mail | |
| Notes | |

| | |
|---|---|
| Type | Geographic |
| Major | All |
| Scholarship Name | **Schmitt, William E. Foundation, Inc.** |
| City | Evansville |
| Organization | William E. Schmitt Foundation, Inc. |
| Amount | $5000—$10,000 |
| Annual/One-Time | One Time |
| Requirements | Student must be between the ages of 16—20, and be enrolled full-time or part-time at an accredited U.S. college university. Must complete a formal application. |
| Deadline | March |
| Contact Name | William E. Schmitt Foundation, Inc. |
| Address | 4445 Commerce Street |
| State | IN |
| Zip Code | 47710 |
| Phone | |
| Fax | |
| E-mail | |
| Notes | |

| | |
|---|---|
| Type | Geographic |
| Major | All |
| Scholarship Name | Showboat Marina Casino Scholarship |
| City | Gary |
| Organization | Indiana University Northwest |
| Amount | Contact Financial Aid Director |
| Annual/One-Time | One Time |
| Requirements | The scholarship is awarded to students with a least 26 credit hours and a GPA of 3.0. Preference is given to students from East Chicago. |
| Deadline | Contact Financial Aid Director |
| Contact Name | Director of Financial Aid |
| Address | Indiana University Northwest 3400 Broadway |
| State | IN |
| Zip Code | 46408 |
| Phone | 219-980-6777 |
| Fax | |
| E-mail | Klantz@iunhaw1.iun.indiana.edu |
| Notes | All students are encouraged to complete a free application for Federal Student Aid (FAFSA). Deadline is March 1. |

| | |
|---|---|
| **Type** | Geographic |
| **Major** | All |
| **Scholarship Name** | **St. John Chamber of Commerce** |
| **City** | St. John |
| **Organization** | St. John Chamber of Commerce |
| **Amount** | $500 |
| **Annual/One-Time** | One Time |
| **Requirements** | Financial need and scholastic ability. |
| **Deadline** | April |
| **Contact Name** | St. John Chamber of Commerce |
| **Address** | 8620 Wicker Blvd. |
| P.O. Box 592 | |
| **State** | IN |
| **Zip Code** | 46373 |
| **Phone** | 219-365-4686 |
| **Fax** | 219-365-4602 |
| **E-mail** | |
| **Notes** | |

| | |
|---|---|
| Type | Geographic |
| Major | All |
| Scholarship Name | **St. John's Lion Club** |
| City | St. John |
| Organization | St. John's Lion Club |
| Amount | $500 |
| Annual/One-Time | One Time |
| Requirements | Students from the town of St. John and surrounding area. |
| Deadline | May |
| Contact Name | St. John Lions Club |
| Address | P.O. Box 331 |
| State | IN |
| Zip Code | 46373-0331 |
| Phone | 219-365-4561 |
| Fax | |
| E-mail | |
| Notes | |

| | |
|---|---|
| Type | Geographic |
| Major | All |
| Scholarship Name | The Everen Scholarship |
| City | Gary |
| Organization | Gary Educational Development Foundation |
| Amount | $1800 |
| Annual/One-Time | One Time |
| Requirements | The graduating senior must be a resident of the Gary Housing Authority conventional apartment units. The student must have a positive high school experience, demonstrated qualities of leadership and citizenship, a reasonable conception of goals and appropriate educational plan including institution of choice and program of study. |
| Deadline | April |
| Contact Name | High School Guidance Counselor or |
| Address | The Gary Educational Development Foundation 3757 W. 21st Ave. |
| State | IN |
| Zip Code | 46404 |
| Phone | 219-977-2192 |
| Fax | 219-977-6258 |
| E-mail | |
| Notes | The scholarship pays $1800 each year to a student until 2006. |

| | |
|---|---|
| Type | Geographic |
| Major | All |
| Scholarship Name | The Gary Housing Authority Commissioner's Scholarship |
| City | Gary |
| Organization | Gary Educational Development Foundation |
| Amount | $800 |
| Annual/One-Time | One Time |
| Requirements | The Graduating senior must be a resident of the Gary Housing Authority conventional apartment units. They must have a good record of positive achievements and school experiences; have demonstrated positive qualities of leadership and citizenship, have a reasonable conception of goals. |
| Deadline | April |
| Contact Name | High School Guidance Counselor or |
| Address | The Gary Educational Development Foundation 3757 W. 21st Ave. |
| State | IN |
| Zip Code | 46404 |
| Phone | 219-977-2192 |
| Fax | 219-977-6258 |
| E-mail | |
| Notes | |

| | |
|---|---|
| Type | Geographic |
| Major | All |
| Scholarship Name | The Mayor's Scholarship |
| City | Gary |
| Organization | Gary Educational Development Foundation |
| Amount | $800 |
| Annual/One-Time | One Time |
| Requirements | The graduating senior must be a resident of the Gary Housing Authority in a conventional apartment unit. Must have a positive high school experience that led to a successful pursuit of goals; have positive qualities of leadership and citizenship; a conception of goals and an appropriate post-secondary educational plan. |
| Deadline | April |
| Contact Name | High School Guidance Counselor of |
| Address | The Gary Educational Development Foundation 3757 W. 21st Ave. |
| State | IN |
| Zip Code | 46404 |
| Phone | 219-977-2192 |
| Fax | 219-977-6258 |
| E-mail | |
| Notes | |

| | |
|---|---|
| Type | Geographic |
| Major | All |
| Scholarship Name | Thomas, Al Scholarship |
| City | Gary |
| Organization | Gary Educational Development Foundation |
| Amount | $800 |
| Annual/One-Time | One Time |
| Requirements | The graduating senior must be a resident in the Gary Housing Authority conventional apartment unit. The student must have a record of positive high school experiences and achievements that will lead to the successful pursuit of selected goals, have demonstrated positive qualities of leadership. |
| Deadline | April |
| Contact Name | High School Guidance Counselor or |
| Address | The Gary Educational Development Foundation 3757 W. 21st Ave. |
| State | IN |
| Zip Code | 46404 |
| Phone | 219-977-2192 |
| Fax | 219-977-6258 |
| E-mail | |
| Notes | |

| | |
|---|---|
| Type | Geographic |
| Major | All |
| Scholarship Name | Tri-Kappa Scholarship |
| City | Hammond |
| Organization | Purdue University Calumet |
| Amount | Contact the Financial Aid Office |
| Annual/One-Time | One Time |
| Requirements | Students must be a Hammond resident with a combined SAT score of 1200, in the top 10% of the class and a GPA of 3.0 and enrolled in 12 hours. All levels of students may apply. |
| Deadline | March |
| Contact Name | Office of Financial Aid |
| Address | Purdue University Calumet<br>2200 169th Street |
| State | IN |
| Zip Code | 46323-2094 |
| Phone | 219-989-2301 |
| Fax | 219-989-2771 |
| E-mail | finaid@calumet.purdue.edu |
| Notes | Students must complete a Merit Scholarship Application. |

| | |
|---|---|
| Type | Geographic |
| Major | All |
| Scholarship Name | U.S Steel Scholars Award |
| City | Pittsburgh |
| Organization | USX Foundation |
| Amount | $20,000 (over a four-year period) |
| Annual/One-Time | One Time |
| Requirements | The student must be a graduate of a Gary high school with high academic achievement. |
| Deadline | Contact Foundation |
| Contact Name | U.S. Steel Scholars Award |
| Address | USX Foundation |
| | 600 Grant Street -RM 685 |
| State | PA |
| Zip Code | 15219-4776 |
| Phone | 412-433-5237 |
| Fax | |
| E-mail | |
| Notes | |

| | |
|---|---|
| **Type** | Geographic |
| **Major** | All |
| **Scholarship Name** | Vancom/Calumet Bus Service Scholarship |
| **City** | Gary |
| **Organization** | Gary Educational Development Foundation |
| **Amount** | $800 |
| **Annual/One-Time** | One Time |
| **Requirements** | The graduating senior must be a student at a Gary high school and must pursue a career path that can be competed in one or two years. Trade, vocational, business, tow year colleges and all proprietary schools apply. The student must have high qualities of character and a good high school record of experiences and achievements. |
| **Deadline** | April |
| **Contact Name** | High School Guidance Counselor of |
| **Address** | The Gary Educational Development Foundation 3757 W. 21st Ave. |
| **State** | IN |
| **Zip Code** | 46404 |
| **Phone** | 219-977-2192 |
| **Fax** | 219-977-6258 |
| **E-mail** | |
| **Notes** | |

| | |
|---|---|
| Type | Geographic |
| Major | All |
| Scholarship Name | Watkins Shell/New Mount Moriah Baptist Church |
| City | Gary |
| Organization | Gary Educational Development Foundation |
| Amount | $700 |
| Annual/One-Time | One Time |
| Requirements | The graduating senior must be a student at a Gary high school, has a record of service to the community, school and church, be active in a Baptist church, has positive qualities observed directly or by references, has an appropriate education plan including institution and study program and financial need. Preference given to New Mt. Moriah members. |
| Deadline | April |
| Contact Name | High School Guidance Counselor or |
| Address | The Gary Educational Development Foundation 3757 W. 21st Ave. |
| State | IN |
| Zip Code | 46404 |
| Phone | 219-977-2192 |
| Fax | 219-977-6258 |
| E-mail | |
| Notes | |

| | |
|---|---|
| Type | Geographic |
| Major | All |
| Scholarship Name | Wirt, William A. Scholarship (All Gary High Schools) |
| City | Gary |
| Organization | Gary Educational Development Foundation |
| Amount | $400 |
| Annual/One-Time | One Time |
| Requirements | Must be a graduating senior from one of six Gary high schools and M.L. King Academy. The recipient must be enrolled with a schedule of at least eight (8) semester hours in an area learning center or full-time college campus. This award is in addition to all other financial aid a student may receive and can be spent on related school needs. |
| Deadline | April |
| Contact Name | High School Guidance Counselor or |
| Address | The Gary Educational Development Foundation 3757 W. 21st Ave. |
| State | IN |
| Zip Code | 46404 |
| Phone | 219-977-2192 |
| Fax | 219-977-6258 |
| E-mail | |
| Notes | |

| | |
|---|---|
| Type | Geographic |
| Major | All |
| Scholarship Name | Wright, Thomas T. Scholarship |
| City | Gary |
| Organization | Gary Educational Development Foundation |
| Amount | $1000 |
| Annual/One-Time | One Time |
| Requirements | Must be a senior from a Gary high school, have been accepted at an accredited college or university, have a 3.0 GPA, show high qualities of character and service and is currently a member of a Christian church. A letter from the church pastor is required. Also must have demonstrated financial need. |
| Deadline | April |
| Contact Name | High School Guidance Counselor or |
| Address | The Gary Educational Development Foundation 3757 W. 21st Ave. |
| State | IN |
| Zip Code | 46404 |
| Phone | 219-977-2192 |
| Fax | 219-977-6258 |
| E-mail | |
| Notes | |

| | |
|---|---|
| Type | Geographic |
| Major | All (Foreign Affairs preferable) |
| Scholarship Name | Gary Rotary Club/Ban Yarrington |
| City | Gary |
| Organization | Gary Educational Development Foundation |
| Amount | $800 |
| Annual/One-Time | One Time |
| Requirements | The graduating senior must be a student at a Gary high school. Student must have high academic accomplishments, demonstrated high qualities of character and service, a record of achievements consistent with a successful pursuit of selected goals and positive qualities observed directly or through references. |
| Deadline | April |
| Contact Name | High School Guidance Counselor or |
| Address | The Gary Educational Development Foundation 3757 W. 21st Ave. |
| State | IN |
| Zip Code | 46404 |
| Phone | 219-977-2192 |
| Fax | 219-977-6258 |
| E-mail | |
| Notes | |

| | |
|---|---|
| Type | Geographic |
| Major | Architectural Engineering Technology |
| Scholarship Name | Carras-Szany & Associates Scholarship |
| City | Hammond |
| Organization | Purdue University Calumet |
| Amount | Contact Financial Aid Office |
| Annual/One-Time | One Time |
| Requirements | The student must be an incoming Freshman with a combined SAT score of 800 and a GPA of 3.0. The student must reside in Lake/Porter counties. |
| Deadline | March 1 |
| Contact Name | Office of Financial Aid |
| Address | Purdue University Calumet 2200 169th Street |
| State | IN |
| Zip Code | 46323-2094 |
| Phone | 219-989-2301 |
| Fax | 219-989-2771 |
| E-mail | finaid@calumet.purdue.edu |
| Notes | All students are encouraged to complete a free application for Federal Student Aid (FAFSA). Deadline is March 1. |

| | |
|---|---|
| Type | Geographic |
| Major | Business management, Marketing, Retail |
| Scholarship Name | Strack Family Scholarship |
| City | Gary |
| Organization | Indiana University Northwest |
| Amount | Contact Financial Aid Director |
| Annual/One-Time | One Time |
| Requirements | The student must live in the Strack and Van Til Supermarkets' area. Preference given to employees or their children. Recipients must have a 2.8 GPA and demonstrated financial need. |
| Deadline | Contact Director of Financial |
| Contact Name | Director of Financial Aid |
| Address | Indiana University Northwest 3400 Broadway |
| State | IN |
| Zip Code | 46408 |
| Phone | 219-980-6777 |
| Fax | |
| E-mail | Klantz@iunhaw1.iun.indiana.edu |
| Notes | All students are encouraged to complete a free application for Federal Student Aid (FAFSA). Deadline is March 1. |

| | |
|---|---|
| Type | Geographic |
| Major | Computer Technology |
| Scholarship Name | Maniotes, Sam & John Scholarship |
| City | Hammond |
| Organization | Purdue University Calumet |
| Amount | Contact Financial Aid Office |
| Annual/One-Time | One Time |
| Requirements | The student must be a sophomore, junior or senior with a GPA of 2.5 and enrolled with at least 12 credit hours. The student must also be a resident of Hammond, IN. |
| Deadline | March |
| Contact Name | Office of Financial Aid |
| Address | Purdue University Calumet 2200 169th Street |
| State | IN |
| Zip Code | 46323-2094 |
| Phone | 219-989-2301 |
| Fax | 219-989-2771 |
| E-mail | finaid@calumet.purdue.edu |
| Notes | Student must complete the Free Application for Student Financial Aid (FAFSA) and the Merit Scholarship Application. |

| | |
|---|---|
| Type | Geographic |
| Major | Construction Technology, Building |
| Scholarship Name | Powers and Sons Construction Company, Inc. |
| City | Gary |
| Organization | Gary Educational Development Foundation |
| Amount | $6000 |
| Annual/One-Time | One Time |
| Requirements | The graduating senior must be a student at a Gary high school. The student must have a career plan, a good record of high school achievements, displays positive personal qualities, has demonstrated qualities of leadership and good citizenship either observed or through references. |
| Deadline | April |
| Contact Name | High School Guidance Counselor or |
| Address | The Gary Educational Development Foundation 3757 W. 21st Ave. |
| State | IN |
| Zip Code | 46404 |
| Phone | 219-977-2192 |
| Fax | 219-977-6258 |
| E-mail | |
| Notes | |

| | |
|---|---|
| Type | Geographic |
| Major | Dance/Drama Performance |
| Scholarship Name | Tri- Kappa Fine Arts Scholarship |
| City | Schererville |
| Organization | Tri-Kappa Fine Arts Scholarship Fund |
| Amount | $750 |
| Annual/One-Time | One Time |
| Requirements | Sophomore and Junior students who are enrolled in Dance/Drama and are planning to perform in their field. Must be residents of Crown Point. |
| Deadline | January |
| Contact Name | Jennifer Sobek, Scholarship Committee |
| Address | Tri-Kappa Key Scholarship |
| State | IN |
| Zip Code | 46375 |
| Phone | 219-738-1817 |
| Fax | |
| E-mail | |
| Notes | Application of Tri-Kappa Key Scholarship must be completed. |

| | |
|---|---|
| Type | Geographic |
| Major | Education |
| Scholarship Name | Smith, Charles O. and Mary Scholarship |
| City | Gary |
| Organization | Gary Educational Development Foundation |
| Amount | $800 |
| Annual/One-Time | One Time |
| Requirements | The graduating senior must be a student at a Gary high school and demonstrate high qualities of character and service, displays positive personal qualities, and an identifiable record of financial need. |
| Deadline | April |
| Contact Name | High School Guidance Counselor or |
| Address | The Gary Educational Development Foundation 3757 W. 21st Ave. |
| State | IN |
| Zip Code | 46404 |
| Phone | 219-977-2192 |
| Fax | 219-977-6258 |
| E-mail | |
| Notes | |

| | |
|---|---|
| Type | Geographic |
| Major | Education (English and Literature) |
| Scholarship Name | Shropshire, Sadie Williams Educational Scholarship |
| City | Gary |
| Organization | Gary Educational Development Foundation |
| Amount | $600 |
| Annual/One-Time | One Time |
| Requirements | The graduating senior must be a student at a Gary high school and is community oriented. The student must have demonstrated excellence of character and leadership in service, has a cumulative GPA of C-plus of better and has demonstrated the ability to set a goal and work toward its achievement. |
| Deadline | April |
| Contact Name | High School Guidance Counselor or |
| Address | The Gary Educational Development Foundation 3757 W. 21st Ave. |
| State | IN |
| Zip Code | 46404 |
| Phone | 219-977-2192 |
| Fax | 219-977-6258 |
| E-mail | |
| Notes | |

| | |
|---|---|
| Type | Geographic |
| Major | Education, Special Education |
| Scholarship Name | Williams, Clara Lofton Scholarship |
| City | Gary |
| Organization | Gary Educational Development Foundation |
| Amount | $2000 (divided into four years) |
| Annual/One-Time | One Time |
| Requirements | Must be a graduating senior planning a career in education with preference given to special education, demonstrated leadership, scholarship and service. The recipient must maintain a GPA of 2.0 or better for the duration of the scholarship. |
| Deadline | April |
| Contact Name | High School Guidance Counselor or |
| Address | The Gary Educational Development Foundation 3757 W. 21st Ave. |
| State | IN |
| Zip Code | 46404 |
| Phone | 219-977-2192 |
| Fax | 219-977-6258 |
| E-mail | |
| Notes | Scholarship rotates: 2004—West Side; 2008—Horace Mann; 2012—Emerson; 2016—Roosevelt; 2020—L. Wallace; 2024—Wirt. |

| | |
|---|---|
| Type | Geographic |
| Major | English or English Literature |
| Scholarship Name | Rowley, Fred C. and Lois E. Scholarship |
| City | Gary |
| Organization | Indiana University Northwest |
| Amount | Contact Financial Aid Director |
| Annual/One-Time | One Time |
| Requirements | The scholarship is given to students who are juniors with a GPA of 3.0. Preference is given to students who are residents of Hammond or Munster. |
| Deadline | Contact Financial Aid Director |
| Contact Name | Director of Financial Aid |
| Address | Indiana University Northwest<br>3400 Broadway |
| State | IN |
| Zip Code | 46408 |
| Phone | 219-980-6777 |
| Fax | |
| E-mail | Klantz@iunhaw1.iun.indiana.edu |
| Notes | All students are encouraged to complete a free application for Federal Student Aid (FAFSA). Deadline is March 1. |

| | |
|---|---|
| Type | Geographic |
| Major | Foreign language |
| Scholarship Name | McCullough, Frankie Woods Foreign Language/Travel Award |
| City | Gary |
| Organization | Gary Educational Development Foundation |
| Amount | $500 |
| Annual/One-Time | One Time |
| Requirements | The graduating senior must be a student at a Gary high school and have the intent to continue foreign language study, maintain a C+ or better average in the foreign language studied and have studied a single foreign language for at least three years or two foreign languages for at least two years each. |
| Deadline | April |
| Contact Name | High School Guidance Counselor or |
| Address | The Gary Educational Development Foundation 3757 W. 21st Ave. |
| State | IN |
| Zip Code | 46404 |
| Phone | 219-977-2192 |
| Fax | 219-977-6258 |
| E-mail | |
| Notes | A travel stipend is available for the senior year in high school. |

| | |
|---|---|
| Type | Geographic |
| Major | Medical and Nursing Education |
| Scholarship Name | Westhaysen, Peter V. Medical Trust |
| City | Hammond |
| Organization | Peter V. Westhaysen Medical Education |
| Amount | $500—$1000 |
| Annual/One-Time | One Time |
| Requirements | Residents of Lake County attending an accredited college or university. Application required. |
| Deadline | June |
| Contact Name | Peter V. Westhaysen Medical Education Trust |
| Address | c/o Bank Calumet P.O. Box 69 |
| State | IN |
| Zip Code | 46320 |
| Phone | 219-932-6900 |
| Fax | |
| E-mail | |
| Notes | |

| | |
|---|---|
| Type | Geographic |
| Major | Music |
| Scholarship Name | LaPorte Amateur Musical Club Scholarship |
| City | Michigan City |
| Organization | Unity Foundation of LaPorte County, Inc. |
| Amount | Up to $500 |
| Annual/One-Time | One Time |
| Requirements | Must be a legal resident of LaPorte County and a graduate of LaPorte High School. Must be studying music and striving to obtain an undergraduate, graduate or doctoral degree. |
| Deadline | April 15 |
| Contact Name | Unity Foundation of LaPorte County, Inc. |
| Address | P.O. Box 527 |
| State | IN |
| Zip Code | 46361 |
| Phone | 219-879-0327 |
| Fax | |
| E-mail | |
| Notes | |

| | |
|---|---|
| Type | Geographic |
| Major | Pharmacy/Health |
| Scholarship Name | Lyles, Evette Pharm. D./KMBC Scholarship |
| City | Gary |
| Organization | Gary Educational Development Foundation |
| Amount | $800 |
| Annual/One-Time | One Time |
| Requirements | The graduating senior must be a student at a Gary high school. The student must have a GPA of 2.5 or better, combined SAT scores of 800+ or ACT of 18+, reflect higher level math and science classes. Priority given to members of Koinonia Baptist Church and Emerson VPA School. |
| Deadline | April |
| Contact Name | High School Guidance Counselor or |
| Address | The Gary Educational Development Foundation 3757 W. 21st Ave. |
| State | IN |
| Zip Code | 46404 |
| Phone | 219-977-2192 |
| Fax | 219-977-6258 |
| E-mail | |
| Notes | All students are encouraged to complete a free application for Federal Student Aid (FAFSA). Deadline is March 1. |

| | |
|---|---|
| Type | Geographic |
| Major | Physical Therapy |
| Scholarship Name | Tolin, Joyce Physical Therapy Assistant Scholarship |
| City | Gary |
| Organization | Gary Educational Development Foundation |
| Amount | $800 |
| Annual/One-Time | One Time |
| Requirements | The graduating senior must be a student at a Gary high school and upon graduating from a post-secondary institution provide two (2) years of service to The Methodist Hospitals. The recipient must have a junior or senior GPA of 2.0 or above, high qualities of service and character and interest in health sciences. |
| Deadline | April |
| Contact Name | High School Guidance Counselor or |
| Address | The Gary Educational Development Foundation 3757 W. 21st Ave. |
| State | IN |
| Zip Code | 46404 |
| Phone | 219-977-2192 |
| Fax | 219-977-6258 |
| E-mail | |
| Notes | |

| | |
|---|---|
| Type | Geographic |
| Major | Real Estate or related business field |
| Scholarship Name | Gary Board of Realtors/Greater N.W.I. Association |
| City | Gary |
| Organization | Gary Educational Development Foundation |
| Amount | $700 |
| Annual/One-Time | One Time |
| Requirements | The graduating senior must attend a Gary high school and have a career goal and a record of positive high school experiences. |
| Deadline | April |
| Contact Name | High School Guidance Counselor or |
| Address | The Gary Educational Development Foundation 3757 W. 21st Ave. |
| State | IN |
| Zip Code | 46404 |
| Phone | 219-977-2192 |
| Fax | 219-977-6258 |
| E-mail | |
| Notes | |

| | |
|---|---|
| **Type** | Geographic |
| **Major** | Science |
| **Scholarship Name** | Oliver, Montague Dr. Scholarship |
| **City** | Gary |
| **Organization** | Gary Educational Development Foundation |
| **Amount** | $800 |
| **Annual/One-Time** | One Time |
| **Requirements** | The graduating senior must be a student at a Gary high school and have career goals, a record of positive high school experiences, achievements consistent with a successful pursuit of selected goals, positive personal qualities as observed directly or through references and a good record of service to school and/or community. |
| **Deadline** | April |
| **Contact Name** | High School Guidance Counselor or |
| **Address** | The Gary Educational Development Foundation 3757 W. 21st Ave. |
| **State** | IN |
| **Zip Code** | 46404 |
| **Phone** | 219-977-2192 |
| **Fax** | 219-977-6258 |
| **E-mail** | |
| **Notes** | |

| | |
|---|---|
| Type | Geographic |
| Major | Telecommunications |
| Scholarship Name | FRED Scholarship |
| City | Hebron |
| Organization | NITCO |
| Amount | Contact NITCO |
| Annual/One-Time | One Time |
| Requirements | Provided educational opportunities for individuals with a deep commitment to their rural communities and desire to return with new knowledge and understanding. Must have telephone exchanges that begin with: 219-988, 219-996, 219-987, 219-345, 219-394 to qualify for this award. |
| Deadline | Contact NITCO |
| Contact Name | Mike Bucko or Don Schoenbeck |
| Address | NITCO P.O. Box 67<br>205 N. Washington |
| State | IN |
| Zip Code | 46341 |
| Phone | 219-996-2981 |
| Fax | |
| E-mail | |
| Notes | Must fill out FRED Scholarship form. |

| | |
|---|---|
| **Type** | Geographic |
| **Major** | The "Helping" Professions |
| **Scholarship Name** | Kaplan, Sharon Scholarship |
| **City** | Gary |
| **Organization** | Gary Educational Development Foundation |
| **Amount** | $500 |
| **Annual/One-Time** | One Time |
| **Requirements** | The graduating senior must be a student at a Gary high school and have a reasonable conception of career goals, a record of positive school experiences and achievements that will lead to goals and high qualities of character and service and displays positive qualities as observed directly or through references. |
| **Deadline** | April |
| **Contact Name** | High School Guidance Counselor of |
| **Address** | The Gary Educational Development Foundation 3757 W. 21st Ave. |
| **State** | IN |
| **Zip Code** | 46404 |
| **Phone** | 219-977-2192 |
| **Fax** | 219-977-6258 |
| **E-mail** | |
| **Notes** | |

# Minority Scholarships

| | |
|---|---|
| Type | Minority |
| Major | All |
| Scholarship Name | **African American Scholarship** |
| City | Hammond |
| Organization | Purdue University Calumet |
| Amount | Contact Financial Aid Office |
| Annual/One-Time | One Time |
| Requirements | African American students with a GPA of 3.0 and enrolled in at least 6 hours. |
| Deadline | March 1 |
| Contact Name | Office of Financial Aid |
| Address | Purdue University Calumet 2200 169th Street |
| State | IN |
| Zip Code | 46323-2094 |
| Phone | 219-989-2301 |
| Fax | 219-989-2771 |
| E-mail | finaid@calumet.purdue.edu |
| Notes | All students are encouraged to complete a free application for Federal Student Aid (FAFSA) and complete a Merit Scholarship form. |

| | |
|---|---|
| Type | Minority |
| Major | All |
| Scholarship Name | Altrusa of the Dunes Scholar Scholarship |
| City | Gary |
| Organization | Indiana University Northwest |
| Amount | $500 |
| Annual/One-Time | One Time |
| Requirements | The award is given to a full- or part-time undergraduate who has attained junior standing with a minimum 2.7 grade-point average. Preference is given to female candidates |
| Deadline | See Financial Aid Director |
| Contact Name | Director of Financial Aid |
| Address | Indiana University Northwest 3400 Broadway |
| State | IN |
| Zip Code | 46408 |
| Phone | 219-980-6777 |
| Fax | |
| E-mail | Klantz@iunhaw1.iun.indiana.edu |
| Notes | All students are encouraged to complete a free application for Federal Student Aid (FAFSA). Deadline is March 1. |

| | |
|---|---|
| Type | Minority |
| Major | All |
| Scholarship Name | Bank One Scholarship |
| City | Gary |
| Organization | Indiana University |
| Amount | Full |
| Annual/One-Time | Annual |
| Requirements | This full-support scholarship is awarded annually to a financially deserving and academically meritorious freshman at IUN with preference given to minorities. The scholarship may be renewed annually providing established academic criteria are satisfied |
| Deadline | March 1 |
| Contact Name | Financial Aid Director |
| Address | Indiana University Northwest 3400 Broadway |
| State | IN |
| Zip Code | 46408 |
| Phone | 219-980-6777 |
| Fax | |
| E-mail | Klantz@iunhaw1.iun.indiana.edu |
| Notes | All students are encouraged to complete a free application for Federal Student Aid (FAFSA). Deadline is March 1. |

| | |
|---|---|
| Type | Minority |
| Major | All |
| Scholarship Name | Black Leaders for Education and Economic Development |
| City | Gary |
| Organization | The Gary Educational Development |
| Amount | $500 |
| Annual/One-Time | One Time |
| Requirements | The graduating senior must be an African-American male at a Gary high school; show qualities of leadership, character, community and church service; must be enrolled at a four year accredited college or university; submit a 250-word essay stating educational goals and interest in becoming a future black leader and prove financial need. |
| Deadline | April |
| Contact Name | High School Guidance Counselor or |
| Address | The Gary Educational Development Foundation 3757 W. 21st Ave. |
| State | IN |
| Zip Code | 46404 |
| Phone | 219 977-2192 |
| Fax | 219-977-6258 |
| E-mail | |
| Notes | |

| | |
|---|---|
| Type | Minority |
| Major | All |
| Scholarship Name | Community Colleges of Indiana (Ivy Tech) |
| City | Gary |
| Organization | Community College of Indiana |
| Amount | Varies |
| Annual/One-Time | One Time |
| Requirements | African American students. Based on financial need. |
| Deadline | June 30 |
| Contact Name | Director of Financial Aid |
| Address | Community Colleges of Indiana 1440 E. 35th Ave. |
| State | IN |
| Zip Code | 46409 |
| Phone | 219-980-1111 |
| Fax | |
| E-mail | |
| Notes | All students are encouraged to complete a free application for Federal Student Aid (FAFSA). Deadline is March 1. |

| | |
|---|---|
| Type | Minority |
| Major | All |
| Scholarship Name | Dinkins, Marcus Antonio |
| City | Gary |
| Organization | Gary Educational Development Foundation |
| Amount | $700 |
| Annual/One-Time | One Time |
| Requirements | The student must be a deserving African-American male graduating from a Gary high school and preparing for a sound career. |
| Deadline | April |
| Contact Name | Gary High School Guidance Counselor or |
| Address | The Gary Educational Development Foundation 3757 W. 21st. Ave. |
| State | IN |
| Zip Code | 46404 |
| Phone | 219-977-2192 |
| Fax | 219-977-6258 |
| E-mail | |
| Notes | |

| | |
|---|---|
| Type | Minority |
| Major | All |
| Scholarship Name | Fernandez, Andrew Memorial Scholarship |
| City | Gary |
| Organization | Indiana University Northwest |
| Amount | $500 |
| Annual/One-Time | One Time |
| Requirements | This scholarship is presented annually to an outstanding student of Hispanic descent. |
| Deadline | See Financial Aid Director |
| Contact Name | Director of Financial Aid |
| Address | Indiana University Northwest 3400 Broadway |
| State | IN |
| Zip Code | 46408 |
| Phone | 219-980-6777 |
| Fax | |
| E-mail | Klantz@iunhaw1.iun.indiana.edu |
| Notes | All students are encouraged to complete a free application for Federal Student Aid (FAFSA). Deadline is March 1. |

| | |
|---|---|
| Type | Minority |
| Major | All |
| Scholarship Name | Gary NAACP Life Membership Committee |
| City | Gary |
| Organization | Gary Educational Development Foundation |
| Amount | $4000 |
| Annual/One-Time | One Time |
| Requirements | The graduating senior must be a minority student in a Gary high school with a good record of high school experiences planning to attend a four year college or university, have achievements that will lead to the successful pursuit of the selected goals, display positive personal qualities. |
| Deadline | April |
| Contact Name | High School Guidance Counselor or |
| Address | The Gary Educational Development Foundation 3757 W. 21st Ave. |
| State | IN |
| Zip Code | 46404 |
| Phone | 219-977-2192 |
| Fax | 219-977-6258 |
| E-mail | |
| Notes | |

| | |
|---|---|
| Type | Minority |
| Major | All |
| Scholarship Name | Gary-Morehouse College Alumni Scholarship |
| City | Gary |
| Organization | Gary Educational Development Foundation |
| Amount | $2000 |
| Annual/One-Time | Annual |
| Requirements | The graduating senior must be an African American male student at a Gary high school. The recipient must display positive personal qualities, have a reasonable conception of his career goals, demonstrates high qualities of character and service and positive personal qualities. |
| Deadline | April |
| Contact Name | High School Guidance Counselor or |
| Address | The Gary Educational Development Foundation 3757 W. 21st Ave. |
| State | IN |
| Zip Code | 46404 |
| Phone | 219-977-2192 |
| Fax | 219-977-6258 |
| E-mail | |
| Notes | |

| | |
|---|---|
| Type | Minority |
| Major | All |
| Scholarship Name | Gomez, Cynthia Scholarship |
| City | Griffith |
| Organization | Sigma Lambda Gamma |
| Amount | Contact Scholarship Fund |
| Annual/One-Time | One Time |
| Requirements | Awards will go to 2 (1 male & 1 female) Purdue Calumet Latin/Minority students between the ages of 17 and 25. The student must have a GPA of 2.5 and be enrolled for 12 hours. An essay is required along with the scholarship application and interview. |
| Deadline | Contact Organization |
| Contact Name | Melissa Ramos or Gina Rodriguez |
| Address | Sigma Lambda Gamma P.O. Box 814 |
| State | IN |
| Zip Code | 46319 |
| Phone | 219-980-9022 or 219-924-6400 |
| Fax | |
| E-mail | |
| Notes | |

| | |
|---|---|
| Type | Minority |
| Major | All |
| Scholarship Name | Hispanic Scholarship |
| City | Hammond |
| Organization | Purdue University Calumet |
| Amount | Contact Financial Aid Office |
| Annual/One-Time | One Time |
| Requirements | Student must be Hispanic. |
| Deadline | March 1 |
| Contact Name | Office of Financial Aid |
| Address | Purdue University Calumet 2200 169th Street |
| State | IN |
| Zip Code | 46323-2094 |
| Phone | 219-989-2301 |
| Fax | 219-989-2771 |
| E-mail | finaid@calumet.purdue.edu |
| Notes | All students are encouraged to complete a free application for Federal Student Aid (FAFSA) and complete a Merit Scholarship form. |

| | |
|---|---|
| Type | Minority |
| Major | All |
| Scholarship Name | Indiana Black Expo Scholarship Program |
| City | Indianapolis |
| Organization | Indiana Black Expo (IBE) |
| Amount | Contact IBE |
| Annual/One-Time | One Time |
| Requirements | Applicants must submit required documents and letters of reference from knowledgeable persons attesting to the applicant's personal achievements, talents and potential. |
| Deadline | Third Friday in April |
| Contact Name | Local Indiana Black Expo Chapter or |
| Address | IBE Scholarship Program<br>3145 N. Meridian Street |
| State | IN |
| Zip Code | 46208 |
| Phone | 317-925-2702 |
| Fax | |
| E-mail | |
| Notes | |

| | |
|---|---|
| Type | Minority |
| Major | All |
| Scholarship Name | Kappa Alpha Psi Fraternity Scholarship |
| City | Gary |
| Organization | Gary Educational Development Foundation |
| Amount | $500 |
| Annual/One-Time | One Time |
| Requirements | Must be a graduating African-American male from a Gary high schools and has been accepted by an accredited college of university. Each Gary high school awards the stipend on a rotational basis. |
| Deadline | April |
| Contact Name | High School Guidance Counselor or |
| Address | The Gary Educational Development Foundation 3757 W. 21st Ave. |
| State | IN |
| Zip Code | 46404 |
| Phone | 219-977-2192 |
| Fax | 219-977-6258 |
| E-mail | |
| Notes | |

| | |
|---|---|
| Type | Minority |
| Major | All |
| Scholarship Name | Mintz Scholarship |
| City | Gary |
| Organization | Indiana University Northwest |
| Amount | $1000 |
| Annual/One-Time | One Time |
| Requirements | The scholarship is awarded to a female student who has demonstrated outstanding academic achievement with at least a 3.0 GPA and a least 25 years of age. The student must have attained junior or senior standing at IUN. |
| Deadline | Contact Financial Aid Director |
| Contact Name | Director of Financial Aid |
| Address | Indiana University Northwest 3400 Broadway |
| State | IN |
| Zip Code | 46408 |
| Phone | 219-980-6777 |
| Fax | |
| E-mail | Klantz@iunhaw1.iun.indiana.edu |
| Notes | All students are encouraged to complete a free application for Federal Student Aid (FAFSA). Deadline is March 1. |

| | |
|---|---|
| Type | Minority |
| Major | All |
| Scholarship Name | NIABSE |
| City | Gary |
| Organization | Gary Educational Development Foundation |
| Amount | $800 |
| Annual/One-Time | One Time |
| Requirements | African American student who is involved in cultural events, such as Dr. Martin Luther King Jr Convocation, Kwanzaa, SABA, etc. |
| Deadline | April |
| Contact Name | High School Guidance Counselor or |
| Address | The Gary Educational Development Foundation 3757 W. 21st Ave. |
| State | IN |
| Zip Code | 46404-2899 |
| Phone | 219-977-2191 |
| Fax | 219-977-6258 |
| E-mail | |
| Notes | |

| | |
|---|---|
| Type | Minority |
| Major | All |
| Scholarship Name | P.E.O. Program for Continuing Education |
| City | Munster |
| Organization | P.E.O. |
| Amount | $1500 |
| Annual/One-Time | One Time |
| Requirements | Provides grants to women whose education has been interrupted. Student must be within 24 consecutive months of completing academic or technical course study. Must have been non-student for 12 or more consecutive months. |
| Deadline | Contact Local Representative |
| Contact Name | Ms. Joan Kaluf |
| Address | Chapter AR<br>8215 Hohman Ave. |
| State | IN |
| Zip Code | 46321 |
| Phone | 219-836-5853 |
| Fax | |
| E-mail | |
| Notes | Must complete P.E.O. Application. |

| | |
|---|---|
| Type | Minority |
| Major | All |
| Scholarship Name | **Stanton, Shirley Memorial Award** |
| City | Hammond |
| Organization | Purdue University Calumet |
| Amount | Contact Financial Aid Office |
| Annual/One-Time | One Time |
| Requirements | Preference will be given to a female student pursuing a minor in Women's Studies or an Associate of Arts degree with a concentration in Women's Studies. Consideration for those with demonstrated interest in the field through taking courses in Women's Studies. Must have a GPA of 3.0. All level of students may apply. |
| Deadline | March |
| Contact Name | Office of Financial Aid |
| Address | Purdue University Calumet 2200 169th Street |
| State | IN |
| Zip Code | 46323-2094 |
| Phone | 219-989-2301 |
| Fax | 219-989-2771 |
| E-mail | finaid@calumet.purdue.edu |
| Notes | Must complete a Shirley Stanton Memorial Award Application. |

| | |
|---|---|
| Type | Minority |
| Major | Business |
| Scholarship Name | Lowery, Robert Reverend Scholarship |
| City | Gary |
| Organization | Indiana University Northwest |
| Amount | $1500 |
| Annual/One-Time | One Time |
| Requirements | The scholarship is awarded annually to two minority students planning a career in business. |
| Deadline | Contact Director of Financial |
| Contact Name | Director of Financial Aid |
| Address | Indiana University Northwest<br>3400 Broadway |
| State | IN |
| Zip Code | 46408 |
| Phone | (219) 980-6777 |
| Fax | |
| E-mail | Klantz@iunhaw1.iun.indiana.edu |
| Notes | All students are encouraged to complete a free application for Federal Student Aid (FAFSA). Deadline is March 1. |

| | |
|---|---|
| Type | Minority |
| Major | Business |
| Scholarship Name | Urban Ventures Scholarship |
| City | Gary |
| Organization | Gary Educational Development Foundation |
| Amount | $4000 ($1000 per year) |
| Annual/One-Time | Annual |
| Requirements | The graduating minority senior must be a student at a Gary high school with a positive high school experience and achievements consistent with a successful pursuit of career goals, positive personal qualities as observed directly or through references and demonstrated high qualities of character and service. |
| Deadline | April |
| Contact Name | High School Guidance Counselor or |
| Address | Gary Educational Development Foundation<br>3757 W. 21st Ave. |
| State | IN |
| Zip Code | 46404 |
| Phone | 219-977-2192 |
| Fax | 219-977-6258 |
| E-mail | |
| Notes | |

| | |
|---|---|
| Type | Minority |
| Major | Construction Related |
| Scholarship Name | National Association of Women in Construction Chapter 44 |
| City | South Bend |
| Organization | NAWC |
| Amount | $300—$500 |
| Annual/One-Time | One Time |
| Requirements | For women in construction related programs. |
| Deadline | Contact the Scholarship Fund |
| Contact Name | Joyce E. Davis |
| Address | Scholarship Committee Cole Associates, Inc. 2211 E. Jefferson Blvd. |
| State | IN |
| Zip Code | 46615 |
| Phone | 219-236-4400 |
| Fax | |
| E-mail | |
| Notes | |

| | |
|---|---|
| Type | Minority |
| Major | Elementary Education |
| Scholarship Name | Turner, Grant Scholarship |
| City | Gary |
| Organization | Gary Educational Development Foundation |
| Amount | $800 |
| Annual/One-Time | One Time |
| Requirements | The graduating senior must be an African American male at a Gary high school with a record of good citizenship and positive community service, experiences consistent with a pursuit in the selected field and personal qualities as observed directly or through references. |
| Deadline | April |
| Contact Name | High School Guidance Counselor or The Gary Educational Development Foundation |
| Address | |
| 3757 W. 21st Ave. | |
| State | IN |
| Zip Code | 46404 |
| Phone | 219-977-2192 |
| Fax | |
| E-mail | |
| Notes | |

| | |
|---|---|
| Type | Minority |
| Major | Journalism |
| Scholarship Name | Chicago Sun-Times Minority Scholarship and Internship |
| City | Chicago |
| Organization | Chicago Sun-Times |
| Amount | $1500 |
| Annual/One-Time | Annual |
| Requirements | The student must be a minority student interested in a career in print journalism entering the junior year in college, a graduate from a Lake or Porter county high school, or have lived in the area for at least five years. The scholarship also includes a paid internship between the junior and senior year. Award renewable with a 3.0 GPA. |
| Deadline | March |
| Contact Name | Chicago Sun-Times |
| Address | Attn: Assistant to the Executive Editor 401 N. Wabash |
| State | IL |
| Zip Code | 60611 |
| Phone | 312-321-3000 |
| Fax | |
| E-mail | |
| Notes | |

| | |
|---|---|
| **Type** | Minority |
| **Major** | Nursing |
| **Scholarship Name** | Richards, Hilda Scholarship |
| **City** | Gary |
| **Organization** | Indiana University Northwest |
| **Amount** | $1500` |
| **Annual/One-Time** | One Time |
| **Requirements** | The student must be an African American who is a full- or part-time undergraduate in the Division of Nursing. |
| **Deadline** | Contact Financial Aid Director |
| **Contact Name** | Director of Financial Aid |
| **Address** | Indiana University Northwest 3400 Broadway |
| **State** | IN |
| **Zip Code** | 46408 |
| **Phone** | 219-980-6777 |
| **Fax** | |
| **E-mail** | Klantz@iunhaw1.iun.indiana.edu |
| **Notes** | All students are encouraged to complete a free application for Federal Student Aid (FAFSA). Deadline is March 1. |

| | |
|---|---|
| Type | Minority |
| Major | Nursing, Allied Health Sciences, Pre-Med |
| Scholarship Name | Medical Education Scholarship |
| City | Gary |
| Organization | Indiana University Northwest |
| Amount | $1000 |
| Annual/One-Time | Annual |
| Requirements | Awarded to four minority undergraduate students pursuing degrees in the medical field. The award is renewable yearly during the recipient's undergraduate career at IUN, providing established criteria are satisfied. |
| Deadline | Contact Financial Aid Director |
| Contact Name | Director of Financial Aid |
| Address | Indiana University Northwest 3400 Broadway |
| State | IN |
| Zip Code | 46408 |
| Phone | 219-980-6777 |
| Fax | |
| E-mail | Klantz@iunhaw1.iun.indiana.edu |
| Notes | All students are encouraged to complete a free application for Federal Student Aid (FAFSA). Deadline is March 1. |

# Need-Based Scholarhips

| | |
|---|---|
| Type | Need-Based |
| Major | All |
| Scholarship Name | Calumet College of St. Joseph Assistance Grant |
| City | Whiting |
| Organization | Calumet College of St. Joseph |
| Amount | Up to 50% of tuition |
| Annual/One-Time | Annual |
| Requirements | Need-based assistance for traditional classes. Recipient must register for six or more credit hours per semester. |
| Deadline | See Financial Aid Director |
| Contact Name | Financial Aid Director |
| Address | Calumet College of St. Joseph 2400 New York Ave |
| State | IN |
| Zip Code | 46394 |
| Phone | 219-473-7770 |
| Fax | |
| E-mail | finaid@ccsj.edu |
| Notes | All students are encouraged to complete a free application for Federal Student Aid (FAFSA). Deadline is March 1. |

| | |
|---|---|
| Type | Need-Based |
| Major | All |
| Scholarship Name | Elliott, Peggy Gordon Scholarship |
| City | Gary |
| Organization | Indiana University Northwest |
| Amount | Full tuition |
| Annual/One-Time | One Time |
| Requirements | This scholarship provides for one annual full-tuition award to a continuing student who has reached junior or senior status with exemplary scholastic standing. Preference is given to students with financial need. |
| Deadline | See Financial Aid Director |
| Contact Name | Director of Financial Aid |
| Address | Indiana University Northwest 3400 Broadway |
| State | IN |
| Zip Code | 46408 |
| Phone | 219-980-6777 |
| Fax | |
| E-mail | Klantz@iunhaw1.iun.indiana.edu |
| Notes | All students are encouraged to complete a free application for Federal Student Aid (FAFSA). Deadline is March 1. |

| | |
|---|---|
| **Type** | **Need-Based** |
| **Major** | **All** |
| **Scholarship Name** | **Powers, Leolean Scholarship** |
| City | Gary |
| Organization | Gary Educational Development Foundation |
| Amount | $4000 ($1000 each year) |
| Annual/One-Time | Annual |
| Requirements | The graduating senior must be a student at a Gary high school with a GPA of 2.0 and demonstratable financial need. Student must be pursuing a post-secondary education. |
| Deadline | April |
| Contact Name | High School Guidance Counselor or |
| Address | The Gary Educational Development Foundation 3757 W. 21st. Ave. |
| State | IN |
| Zip Code | 46404 |
| Phone | 219-977-2192 |
| Fax | 219-977-6258 |
| E-mail | |
| Notes | |

| | |
|---|---|
| Type | Need-Based |
| Major | All |
| Scholarship Name | T.I.S.-Tichenor Foundation, Inc. |
| City | Bloomington |
| Organization | T.I.S.—Tichenor Foundation, Inc. |
| Amount | $4000 or more |
| Annual/One-Time | One Time |
| Requirements | Financially needy, single resident of Indiana who is a full-time junior or senior undergraduate of Indiana University Bloomington or Ball State University. IU student must have a GPA of 3.25. Ball State student must have a GPA of 3.0. |
| Deadline | Open |
| Contact Name | Martha Tichenor, President |
| Address | T.I.S. Tichenor Foundation, Inc. P.O. Box 669 |
| State | IN |
| Zip Code | 47402 |
| Phone | 812-332-3307 |
| Fax | |
| E-mail | |
| Notes | |

# ORGANIZATIONAL SCHOLARSHIPS

| | |
|---|---|
| Type | Organizational |
| Major | All |
| Scholarship Name | AAL Scholarship |
| City | Valparaiso |
| Organization | Valparaiso University |
| Amount | $500—$1000 |
| Annual/One-Time | One Time |
| Requirements | Undergraduate students who are Lutheran and members of the AAL. Award based on academic achievements and/or financial need. Renewable with a student continuing to show academic progress with at least a 2.0 |
| Deadline | March 1 |
| Contact Name | Director of Admissions |
| Address | Valparaiso University Kretzmann Hall |
| State | IN |
| Zip Code | 46383 |
| Phone | 219-464-5015 or |
| Fax | |
| E-mail | finaid@valpo.edu |
| Notes | All students are encouraged to complete a free application for Federal Student Aid (FAFSA). Deadline is March 1. |

| | |
|---|---|
| Type | Organizational |
| Major | All |
| Scholarship Name | Bethlehem Steel Scholarship |
| City | Bethlehem |
| Organization | Bethlehem Steel Foundation |
| Amount | $1000 |
| Annual/One-Time | One Time |
| Requirements | Children of Bethlehem Steel employees with a minimum 3.0 GPA. |
| Deadline | April 10 |
| Contact Name | Bethlehem Steel Scholarship |
| Address | Bethlehem Steel Corporation 1170 8th Avenue |
| State | PA |
| Zip Code | 18016 |
| Phone | 610-694-2424 |
| Fax | 610-694-6920 |
| E-mail | |
| Notes | |

| | |
|---|---|
| Type | Organizational |
| Major | All |
| Scholarship Name | **Chicago FM Club** |
| City | Newington |
| Organization | Chicago FM Club |
| Amount | $500 |
| Annual/One-Time | One Time |
| Requirements | The award is for freshmen, sophomores, juniors or seniors in the FCC Ninth Call District in high school or graduates who have a licensed amateur radio operators with technician license. The student must be enrolled in a two or four year college or technical institution. Application required along with transcripts. |
| Deadline | February 1 |
| Contact Name | Mary Garcia |
| Address | ARRL Foundation<br>225 Main Street |
| State | CT |
| Zip Code | 06011-4845 |
| Phone | |
| Fax | |
| E-mail | |
| Notes | |

| | |
|---|---|
| Type | Organizational |
| Major | All |
| Scholarship Name | Garner, Syd Scholarship |
| City | Gary |
| Organization | Indiana University Northwest |
| Amount | Full tuition |
| Annual/One-Time | One Time |
| Requirements | This full tuition scholarship is given to Lake County government employees with five or more years of service, or to applicants who are children of county government employees who plan to attend IUN. |
| Deadline | See Financial Aid Director |
| Contact Name | Director of Financial Aid |
| Address | Indiana University Northwest 3400 Broadway |
| State | IN |
| Zip Code | 46408 |
| Phone | 219-980-6777 |
| Fax | |
| E-mail | Klantz@iunhaw1.iun.indiana.edu |
| Notes | All students are encouraged to complete a free application for Federal Student Aid (FAFSA). Deadline is March 1. |

| | |
|---|---|
| Type | Organizational |
| Major | All |
| Scholarship Name | Inland Employees Federal Credit Union Scholarship |
| City | East Chicago |
| Organization | Inland Employees Federal Credit Union |
| Amount | $1000 |
| Annual/One-Time | One Time |
| Requirements | Member of child of a member of IEFCU, rank in upper 1/3 of their class with a minimum of 850 on the SAT. |
| Deadline | May 1 |
| Contact Name | Scholarship Committee |
| Address | Inland Employees Credit Union 4035 Adler St. |
| State | IN |
| Zip Code | 46312 |
| Phone | |
| Fax | |
| E-mail | |
| Notes | |

| | |
|---|---|
| Type | Organizational |
| Major | All |
| Scholarship Name | ISPAT Inland Scholarship Program |
| City | East Chicago |
| Organization | ISPAT/Inland Steel Corporation |
| Amount | Up to $2000 |
| Annual/One-Time | One Time |
| Requirements | Children of Inland Steel employees. |
| Deadline | Contact ISPAT Inland |
| Contact Name | ISPAT Inland, Inc. |
| Address | 3210 Watling St. M.C. 8-125 |
| State | IN |
| Zip Code | 46312 |
| Phone | |
| Fax | |
| E-mail | |
| Notes | |

| | |
|---|---|
| Type | Organizational |
| Major | All |
| Scholarship Name | Lake County Farm Bureau Scholarship |
| City | Crown Point |
| Organization | Lake County Farm Bureau Scholarship |
| Amount | Up to $2000 |
| Annual/One-Time | One Time |
| Requirements | Must be a member of Lake County Farm Bureau, Inc. |
| Deadline | March 1 |
| Contact Name | Lake County Farm Bureau |
| Address | P.O. Box 964 |
| State | IN |
| Zip Code | 46307-0964 |
| Phone | 219-663-1028 |
| Fax | |
| E-mail | |
| Notes | |

| | |
|---|---|
| Type | Organizational |
| Major | All |
| Scholarship Name | **Lutheran Brotherhood** |
| City | Valparaiso |
| Organization | Valparaiso University |
| Amount | $500—$1000 |
| Annual/One-Time | Annual |
| Requirements | Undergraduate students who are Lutherans and members of the Lutheran Brotherhood. The award is renewable with a GPA of 2.0. |
| Deadline | March 1 |
| Contact Name | Director of Financial Aid |
| Address | Valparaiso University Kretzmann Hall |
| State | IN |
| Zip Code | 46383 |
| Phone | 219-464-5015 or |
| Fax | |
| E-mail | finaid@valpo.edu |
| Notes | All students are encouraged to complete a free application for Federal Student Aid (FAFSA). Deadline is March 1. |

| | |
|---|---|
| Type | Organizational |
| Major | All |
| Scholarship Name | Martin Luther Award |
| City | Valparaiso |
| Organization | Valparaiso University |
| Amount | $1000—$3000 |
| Annual/One-Time | Annual |
| Requirements | Undergraduate who is a dependent of a full-time professional Lutheran church worker or have financial need. The scholarship is renewable with a 2.0 GPA. |
| Deadline | March 1 |
| Contact Name | Director of Financial Aid |
| Address | Valparaiso University |
| | Kretzmann Hall |
| State | IN |
| Zip Code | 46383 |
| Phone | 219-464-5015 or |
| Fax | |
| E-mail | finaid@valpo.edu |
| Notes | |

| | |
|---|---|
| Type | Organizational |
| Major | All |
| Scholarship Name | Nash, Kermit B. Achievement Scholarship |
| City | Gary |
| Organization | National Association for Sickle Cell Disease |
| Amount | $5,000 |
| Annual/One-Time | Annual |
| Requirements | Must be an individual with sickle cell disease (individuals with sickle cell trait are not eligible). |
| Deadline | Contact Executive Director |
| Contact Name | Beatchre Strong Executive Director |
| Address | NW Indiana Sickle Cell Foundation 4801 W. 5th Ave |
| State | IN |
| Zip Code | 46406 |
| Phone | 219-949-5310 |
| Fax | |
| E-mail | |
| Notes | |

| | |
|---|---|
| Type | Organizational |
| Major | All |
| Scholarship Name | Northern Indiana Service Company (NIPSCO) Scholarship |
| City | Hammond |
| Organization | Purdue University Calumet |
| Amount | $1,000 |
| Annual/One-Time | One Time |
| Requirements | Available to Purdue Calumet students who are dependent children of Northern Indiana Public Service Company employees, and students with a visual or physical disability. Students must have a 3.0 GPA, combined SAT score of 900 and enrolled in 12 credit hours. |
| Deadline | March 1 |
| Contact Name | Office of Financial Aid |
| Address | Purdue University Calumet 2200 169th Street |
| State | IN |
| Zip Code | 46323-2094 |
| Phone | 219-989-2301 |
| Fax | 219-989-2771 |
| E-mail | finaid@calumet.purdue.edu |
| Notes | Students must complete a Merit Scholarship Application. |

| | |
|---|---|
| Type | Organizational |
| Major | All |
| Scholarship Name | Valparaiso Guild Scholarship |
| City | Valparaiso |
| Organization | Valparaiso University |
| Amount | $2000 |
| Annual/One-Time | Annual |
| Requirements | Undergraduates who are sons and daughters of a Valparaiso University Guild member. The amount is renewable with a 2.0 GPA. |
| Deadline | March 1 |
| Contact Name | Director of Financial Aid |
| Address | Valparaiso University Kretzmann Hall |
| State | IN |
| Zip Code | 46383 |
| Phone | 219-464-5015 or |
| Fax | |
| E-mail | finaid@valpo.edu |
| Notes | All students are encouraged to complete a free application for Federal Student Aid (FAFSA). Deadline is March 1. |

| | |
|---|---|
| Type | Organizational |
| Major | All |
| Scholarship Name | Wal-Mart Associate Scholarship |
| City | Bentonville |
| Organization | Wal-Mart Foundation |
| Amount | $1000 |
| Annual/One-Time | One Time |
| Requirements | A scholarship offered to high school seniors who work for Wal-Mart Stores, Inc. and to those associate's children ineligible for the Walton Foundation Scholarship. This is an academic scholarship and applicants will be judged on the basis of grades, financial need, academic record, and ACT/SAT scores. |
| Deadline | March 1 |
| Contact Name | Local Wal-Mart Store or |
| Address | The Walton Foundation
702 S.N. 8th Street |
| State | AR |
| Zip Code | 72716-8071 |
| Phone | |
| Fax | |
| E-mail | |
| Notes | |

| | |
|---|---|
| Type | Organizational |
| Major | All |
| Scholarship Name | Walton Foundation Scholarship |
| City | Bentonville |
| Organization | Walton Foundation |
| Amount | $6000 (over four years) |
| Annual/One-Time | One Time |
| Requirements | The Walton Foundation Scholarship is awarded to a child of a Wal-Mart Stores, Inc. associate who is employed full time (28 hours per week or more) for one year as of March 1. This is an academic scholarship and applicants will be judged on their grades, financial need, SAT/ACT scores and academic record. |
| Deadline | March 1 |
| Contact Name | Local Wal-Mart Store or |
| Address | The Walton Foundation 702 S.N. 8th Street |
| State | AK |
| Zip Code | 72716-8071 |
| Phone | |
| Fax | |
| E-mail | |

**Notes**

100 scholarships are awarded company wide. Applications are available starting in January from your location's personnel office.

| | |
|---|---|
| Type | Organizational |
| Major | Education |
| Scholarship Name | Gary Teachers' Union Mary Cheever/Angela Hannagan |
| City | Gary |
| Organization | Gary Educational Development Foundation |
| Amount | $700 |
| Annual/One-Time | One Time |
| Requirements | The graduating senior must be a son or daughter of a Gary Community School Corporation employee who is a member in good standing of the union, the child of a deceased or permanently disabled employee who was a member in good standing, have a record of service to the community and/or their school. |
| Deadline | April |
| Contact Name | High School Guidance Counselor or |
| Address | The Gary Educational Development Foundation 3757 W. 21st Ave. |
| State | IN |
| Zip Code | 46404 |
| Phone | 219-977-2192 |
| Fax | 219-977-6258 |
| E-mail | |
| Notes | |

| | |
|---|---|
| Type | Organizational |
| Major | Engineering |
| Scholarship Name | Shorb, Eugene M Scholarship (NIPSCO) |
| City | Hammond |
| Organization | NIPSCO |
| Amount | Contact Director of Financial Aid |
| Annual/One-Time | One Time |
| Requirements | Recipient should be a son or daughter, niece or nephew of a NIPSCO employee with preference given to those with financial need. |
| Deadline | March 1 |
| Contact Name | Office of Financial Aid |
| Address | Purdue University Calumet 2200 169th Street |
| State | IN |
| Zip Code | 46323-2094 |
| Phone | 219-989-2301 |
| Fax | 219-989-2771 |
| E-mail | finaid@calumet.purdue.edu |
| Notes | All students are encouraged to complete a free application for Federal Student Aid (FAFSA) and Merit Scholarship Application. |

| | |
|---|---|
| Type | Organizational |
| Major | Engineering, Metallurgy, Physical Science, Computer |
| Scholarship Name | Association of Iron & Steel Engineers (Chicago District) |
| City | Pittsburgh |
| Organization | Association of Iron & Steel Engineers |
| Amount | $1000 |
| Annual/One-Time | Annual |
| Requirements | The scholarship is available to a student who is either a dependent of the Chicago District (Active/Associate Member) or a student who maintains a Junior Membership. The award will be principally awarded on overall academic achievement with an emphasis on chemistry, mathematics and physics. |
| Deadline | June 15 |
| Contact Name | Vern Jones |
| Address | Chicago District Education Chairman Three Gateway Center, #1900 |
| State | PA |
| Zip Code | 15222 |
| Phone | 219-399-5237 (local number) |
| Fax | |
| E-mail | sections@aise.org |
| Notes | |

# Returning Student Scholarhips

| | |
|---|---|
| Type | Returning Student |
| Major | All |
| Scholarship Name | Calumet College of St. Joseph Alumni Scholarship |
| City | Whiting |
| Organization | Calumet College of St. Joseph |
| Amount | See Financial Aid Director |
| Annual/One-Time | One Time |
| Requirements | For a graduate of Calumet College of St. Joseph with a Bachelor of Arts or Science degree. |
| Deadline | See Financial Aid Director |
| Contact Name | Director of Financial Aid |
| Address | Calumet College of St. Joseph 2400 New York Ave. |
| State | IN |
| Zip Code | 46394 |
| Phone | 219-473-7770 |
| Fax | |
| E-mail | finaid@ccsj.edu |
| Notes | All students are encouraged to complete a free application for Federal Student Aid (FAFSA). Deadline is March 1. |

| | |
|---|---|
| Type | Returning Student |
| Major | All |
| Scholarship Name | Communication 114 Scholarship |
| City | Hammond |
| Organization | Purdue University Calumet |
| Amount | $500 |
| Annual/One-Time | One Time |
| Requirements | Students who receive a grade of "A" in COM 114 have priority consideration for this scholarship. Applicants must have received a minimum grade of "B" in COM 114 to be eligible. |
| Deadline | March 1 |
| Contact Name | Office of Financial Aid |
| Address | Purdue University Calumet<br>2200 169th Street |
| State | IN |
| Zip Code | 46323-2094 |
| Phone | 219-989-2301 |
| Fax | 219-989-2771 |
| E-mail | finaid@calumet.purdue.edu |
| Notes | Students must apply through the Merit Scholarship Application. |

| | |
|---|---|
| Type | Returning Student |
| Major | All |
| Scholarship Name | Paich, Mildred Scholarship |
| City | Gary |
| Organization | Indiana University Northwest |
| Amount | Contact Financial Aid Director |
| Annual/One-Time | One Time |
| Requirements | This scholarship is awarded to a continuing student at IUN who has demonstrated academic excellence. |
| Deadline | Contact Director of Financial |
| Contact Name | Director of Financial Aid |
| Address | Indiana University Northwest 3400 Broadway |
| State | IN |
| Zip Code | 46408 |
| Phone | 219-980-6777 |
| Fax | |
| E-mail | Klantz@iunhaw1.iun.indiana.edu |
| Notes | All students are encouraged to complete a free application for Federal Student Aid (FAFSA). Deadline is March 1. |

| | |
|---|---|
| Type | Returning Student |
| Major | All |
| Scholarship Name | Thomas, Ray and Josephine Scholarship |
| City | Gary |
| Organization | Indiana University Northwest |
| Amount | Varies |
| Annual/One-Time | One Time |
| Requirements | This scholarship is awarded to a returning student who has excelled academically. |
| Deadline | Contact Financial Aid Director |
| Contact Name | Director of Financial Aid |
| Address | Indiana University Northwest 3400 Broadway |
| State | IN |
| Zip Code | 46404 |
| Phone | 219-980-6777 |
| Fax | |
| E-mail | Klantz@iunhaw1.iun.indiana.edu |
| Notes | All students are encouraged to complete a free application for Federal Student Aid (FAFSA). Deadline is March 1. |

| | |
|---|---|
| Type | Returning Student |
| Major | Engineering, Architectural and/or Material Sciences |
| Scholarship Name | ACI-W.R. Grace Fellowship Award |
| City | Hammond |
| Organization | Purdue University Calumet |
| Amount | $3000 |
| Annual/One-Time | One Time |
| Requirements | Anyone who is completing or has completed studies for the bachelor's degree from an accredited program in the areas of engineering, architecture and/or material sciences in concrete and be a full-time first or second-year graduate student. |
| Deadline | January |
| Contact Name | Office of Financial Aid |
| Address | Purdue University Calumet 2200 169th Street |
| State | IN |
| Zip Code | 46323-2094 |
| Phone | 219-989-2301 |
| Fax | 219-989-2271 |
| E-mail | finaid@calumet.purdue.edu |
| Notes | |

| | |
|---|---|
| Type | Returning Student |
| Major | Management |
| Scholarship Name | Nondorf, Claudia Scholarship |
| City | Hammond |
| Organization | Purdue University Calumet |
| Amount | Contact Financial Aid Office |
| Annual/One-Time | One Time |
| Requirements | Recipient should have completed at least two semesters & have 12 credit hours completed. Single parents preferred. |
| Deadline | March 1 |
| Contact Name | Office of Financial Aid |
| Address | Purdue University Calumet<br>2200 169th Street |
| State | IN |
| Zip Code | 46323-2094 |
| Phone | 219-989-2301 |
| Fax | 219-989-2771 |
| E-mail | finaid@calumet.purdue.edu |
| Notes | All students are encouraged to complete a free application for Federal Student Aid (FAFSA). Deadline is March 1. |

| | |
|---|---|
| Type | Returning Student |
| Major | Marketing or Accounting |
| Scholarship Name | Uzelac, George & Associate Scholarship |
| City | Gary |
| Organization | Indiana University Northwest |
| Amount | $400 |
| Annual/One-Time | One Time |
| Requirements | Must be a student who resides in Lake or Porter County and has attained junior or senior status in the Division of Business or Economics. The student must have an overall GPA of 3.3 on a 4.0 scale. |
| Deadline | Contact Financial Aid Director |
| Contact Name | Director of Financial Aid |
| Address | Indiana University Northwest 3400 Broadway |
| State | IN |
| Zip Code | 46404 |
| Phone | 219-980-6777 |
| Fax | |
| E-mail | Klantz@iunhaw1.iun.indiana.edu |
| Notes | All students are encouraged to complete a free application for Federal Student Aid (FAFSA). Deadline is March 1. |

| | |
|---|---|
| Type | Returning Student |
| Major | Mechanical Engineering Technology |
| Scholarship Name | Winnamac Old Auto Club Scholarship |
| City | Hammond |
| Organization | Purdue University Calumet |
| Amount | Contact Financial Aid |
| Annual/One-Time | One Time |
| Requirements | This scholarship is for a junior with a 3.0 GPA with at least 12 credit hours. Interest in automotive engineering and/or design a must. |
| Deadline | Contact Financial Aid |
| Contact Name | Office of Financial Aid |
| Address | Purdue University Calumet 2200 169th Street |
| State | IN |
| Zip Code | 46323-2094 |
| Phone | 219-989-2301 |
| Fax | 219-989-2771 |
| E-mail | finaid@calumet.purdue.edu |
| Notes | Student must complete the Federal Student Aid form and the Purdue Calumet Merit Scholarship Application. |

| | |
|---|---|
| Type | Returning Student |
| Major | Medical |
| Scholarship Name | Kelly/Prentiss Scholarship |
| City | Michigan City |
| Organization | IMS Investment Management |
| Amount | Up to $1000 |
| Annual/One-Time | One Time |
| Requirements | LaPorte County resident that has satisfactorily completed three years in an accredited medical college or university. Selection will be based upon financial need. |
| Deadline | May 1 |
| Contact Name | Stephanie Oberlie |
| Address | IMS Investment Management P.O. Box 1125 |
| State | IN |
| Zip Code | 46361 |
| Phone | 219-874-9268 |
| Fax | |
| E-mail | |
| Notes | |

| | |
|---|---|
| Type | Returning Student |
| Major | Nursing |
| Scholarship Name | Ellis, Joyce Dr. Graduate Nursing Scholarship |
| City | Hammond |
| Organization | Purdue University Calumet |
| Amount | Contact Director of Financial Aid |
| Annual/One-Time | One Time |
| Requirements | Must have a graduate classification in Nursing, a GPA of 3.75 an be enrolled in 6 hours of graduate hours. |
| Deadline | March 1 |
| Contact Name | Office of Financial Aid |
| Address | Purdue University Calumet 2200 169th Street |
| State | IN |
| Zip Code | 46323-2094 |
| Phone | 219-989-2301 |
| Fax | 219-989-2771 |
| E-mail | finaid@calumet.purdue.edu |
| Notes | Merit Scholarship Application required. |

# SCHOOL-BASED SCHOLARHIPS

| | |
|---|---|
| Type | School-Based |
| Major | All |
| Scholarship Name | Anderson, Warren M. Scholarship |
| City | Gary |
| Organization | Gary Educational Development Foundation |
| Amount | $700 |
| Annual/One-Time | One Time |
| Requirements | The graduating senior must be a student at Gary Roosevelt High School. The student must show exemplary scholastic achievements, demonstrated high qualities of character and leadership, has a record of service, positive personal qualities observed through references and a post-secondary education plan. |
| Deadline | April |
| Contact Name | High School Guidance Counselor or |
| Address | The Gary Educational Development Foundation 3757 W. 21st Ave. |
| State | IN |
| Zip Code | 46404 |
| Phone | 219 977-2192 |
| Fax | 219-977-6258 |
| E-mail | |
| Notes | |

| | |
|---|---|
| Type | School-Based |
| Major | All |
| Scholarship Name | Barnes, Anner H. Scholarship |
| City | Gary |
| Organization | The Gary Educational Development |
| Amount | $700 |
| Annual/One-Time | One Time |
| Requirements | The student must be a student at Gary West Side High School, have demonstrated qualities of service to church (with letters of reference), school and community. Have exemplary scholastic achievement, and complete an essay of no more than 150 words on the question: "What is most important in my life and why". |
| Deadline | April |
| Contact Name | High School Guidance Counselor or |
| Address | The Gary Educational Development Foundation 3757 W. 21st Ave. |
| State | IN |
| Zip Code | 46404 |
| Phone | 219 977-2192 |
| Fax | 219-977-6258 |
| E-mail | |
| Notes | |

| | |
|---|---|
| Type | School-Based |
| Major | All |
| Scholarship Name | Bianco, Sam Scholarship |
| City | Gary |
| Organization | Gary Educational Development Foundation |
| Amount | $800 |
| Annual/One-Time | One Time |
| Requirements | For a Lew Wallace High School graduating senior with a reasonable conception of his/her career goals. |
| Deadline | April |
| Contact Name | High School Guidance Counselor or |
| Address | The Gary Educational Development Foundation 3757 W. 21st. Ave. |
| State | IN |
| Zip Code | 46404 |
| Phone | 219-977-2192 |
| Fax | 219-977-6258 |
| E-mail | |
| Notes | |

| | |
|---|---|
| Type | School-Based |
| Major | All |
| Scholarship Name | **Calumet Child Care Scholarship** |
| City | Hammond |
| Organization | Purdue University Calumet |
| Amount | Contact Financial Aid |
| Annual/One-Time | One Time |
| Requirements | Must have a child at the Purdue Child Care Center. Applications available at the Child Care Center. |
| Deadline | March 1 |
| Contact Name | Purdue Child Care Center |
| Address | Purdue University Calumet<br>2200 169th Street |
| State | IN |
| Zip Code | 46232-2094 |
| Phone | 219-989-2301 |
| Fax | 219-989-2771 |
| E-mail | finaid@calumet.purdue.edu |
| Notes | All students are encouraged to complete a free application for Federal Student Aid (FAFSA). Deadline is March 1. |

| | |
|---|---|
| Type | School-Based |
| Major | All |
| Scholarship Name | **Calumet College of St. Joseph Degree Completion Scholarship** |
| City | Whiting |
| Organization | Calumet College of St. Joseph |
| Amount | See Financial Aid Director |
| Annual/One-Time | One Time |
| Requirements | For Degree Completion students only. |
| Deadline | See Financial Aid Director |
| Contact Name | Director of Financial Aid |
| Address | Calumet College of St. Joseph 2400 New York Ave. |
| State | IN |
| Zip Code | 46394 |
| Phone | 219-473-7770 |
| Fax | |
| E-mail | finaid@ccsj.edu |
| Notes | All students are encouraged to complete a free application for Federal Student Aid (FAFSA). Deadline is March 1. |

| | |
|---|---|
| Type | School-Based |
| Major | All |
| Scholarship Name | Calumet College of St. Joseph Early Admissions Scholarship |
| City | Whiting |
| Organization | Calumet College of St. Joseph |
| Amount | 50% of tuition |
| Annual/One-Time | One Time |
| Requirements | For high school juniors and seniors who take up to two classes per semester. Recipients should have a suggested 3.0 GPA and permission of high school counselor. |
| Deadline | See Financial Aid Director |
| Contact Name | Director of Financial Aid |
| Address | Calumet College of St. Joseph 2400 New York Ave. |
| State | IN |
| Zip Code | 46394 |
| Phone | 219-473-7770 |
| Fax | |
| E-mail | finaid@ccsj.edu |
| Notes | All students are encouraged to complete a free application for Federal Student Aid (FAFSA). Deadline is March 1. |

| | |
|---|---|
| Type | School-Based |
| Major | All |
| Scholarship Name | **Calumet College of St. Joseph Gary and Diocese Grants** |
| City | Whiting |
| Organization | Calumet College of St. Joseph |
| Amount | 50% of tuition |
| Annual/One-Time | One Time |
| Requirements | For students in traditional classes only. |
| Deadline | See Financial Aid Director |
| Contact Name | Director of Financial Aid |
| Address | Calumet College of St. Joseph 2400 New York Ave. |
| State | IN |
| Zip Code | 46394 |
| Phone | 219-473-7770 |
| Fax | |
| E-mail | finaid@ccsj.edu |
| Notes | All students are encouraged to complete a free application for Federal Student Aid (FAFSA). Deadline is March 1. |

| | |
|---|---|
| Type | School-Based |
| Major | All |
| Scholarship Name | Calumet College of St. Joseph GED Scholarship |
| City | Whiting |
| Organization | Calumet College of St. Joseph |
| Amount | 50% of tuition |
| Annual/One-Time | One Time |
| Requirements | For students with an average GED score of 50 to 59.9 and a 3.00 or higher semester GPA and register for six or more credit hours per semester in traditional classes. |
| Deadline | See Financial Aid Director |
| Contact Name | Director of Financial Aid |
| Address | Calumet College of St. Joseph 2400 New York Ave. |
| State | IN |
| Zip Code | 46394 |
| Phone | 219-473-7770 |
| Fax | |
| E-mail | finaid@ccsj.edu |
| Notes | All students are encouraged to complete a free application for Federal Student Aid (FAFSA). Deadline is March 1. |

| | |
|---|---|
| Type | School-Based |
| Major | All |
| Scholarship Name | **Calumet College of St. Joseph GED Scholarship** |
| City | Whiting |
| Organization | Calumet College of St. Joseph |
| Amount | 75% of tuition |
| Annual/One-Time | One Time |
| Requirements | Provides 75% of tuition for students with an average GED score of 60 to 69.9 and a 3.50 or higher semester GPA in traditional classes. Recipient must register for is or more credit hours per semester. |
| Deadline | See Financial Aid Director |
| Contact Name | Director of Financial Aid |
| Address | Calumet College of St. Joseph 2400 New York Ave. |
| State | IN |
| Zip Code | 46394 |
| Phone | 219-473-7770 |
| Fax | |
| E-mail | finaid@ccsj.edu |
| Notes | All students are encouraged to complete a free application for Federal Student Aid (FAFSA). Deadline is March 1. |

| | |
|---|---|
| Type | School-Based |
| Major | All |
| Scholarship Name | Calumet College of St. Joseph GED Scholarship |
| City | Whiting |
| Organization | Calumet College of St. Joseph |
| Amount | 100% of tuition |
| Annual/One-Time | One Time |
| Requirements | Student must have an average GED score of 70 or higher and a 3.75 or higher semester GPA. Recipient must register for six or more credit hours per semester in traditional classes. |
| Deadline | See Financial Aid Director |
| Contact Name | Director of Financial Aid |
| Address | Calumet College of St. Joseph 2400 New York Ave. |
| State | IN |
| Zip Code | 46394 |
| Phone | 219-473-7770 |
| Fax | |
| E-mail | finaid@ccsj.edu |
| Notes | All students are encouraged to complete a free application for Federal Student Aid (FAFSA). Deadline is March 1. |

| | |
|---|---|
| Type | School-Based |
| Major | All |
| Scholarship Name | Calumet College of St. Joseph LESS Scholarship |
| City | Whiting |
| Organization | Calumet College of St. Joseph |
| Amount | 33.3%—50% of tuition |
| Annual/One-Time | One Time |
| Requirements | For students 55 years or older. Provides 50% tuition for traditional classes and 33.3% of tuition in the Degree Completion programs. |
| Deadline | See Financial Aid Director |
| Contact Name | Director of Financial Aid |
| Address | Calumet College of St. Joseph 2400 Whiting Ave. |
| State | IN |
| Zip Code | 46394 |
| Phone | 219-473-7770 |
| Fax | |
| E-mail | finaid@ccsj.edu |
| Notes | All students are encouraged to complete a free application for Federal Student Aid (FAFSA). Deadline is March 1. |

| | |
|---|---|
| Type | School-Based |
| Major | All |
| Scholarship Name | Calumet College of St. Joseph Transfer Grant |
| City | Whiting |
| Organization | Calumet College of St. Joseph |
| Amount | $800 full-time, $400 part-time |
| Annual/One-Time | One Time |
| Requirements | Students must transfer a minimum of 60 credit hours or 90 quarter hours to Calumet College of St. Joseph. Students must have a GPA of 2.75 or higher. |
| Deadline | See Financial Aid Director |
| Contact Name | Director of Financial Aid |
| Address | Calumet College of St. Joseph 2400 New York Ave. |
| State | IN |
| Zip Code | 46394 |
| Phone | 219-473-7770 |
| Fax | |
| E-mail | finaid@ccsj.edu |
| Notes | All students are encouraged to complete a free application for Federal Student Aid (FAFSA). Deadline is March 1. |

| | |
|---|---|
| Type | School-Based |
| Major | All |
| Scholarship Name | Carlson, Paul N. —Horace Mann Scholarship |
| City | Gary |
| Organization | Gary Educational Development Foundation |
| Amount | $800 |
| Annual/One-Time | Annual |
| Requirements | The graduating senior must be a student at Horace Mann High School in Gary. The recipient must pursue a four-year degree at a post-secondary institution, possess a GPA of 2.5 or above and demonstrate strong character, work ethic and has a financial need. |
| Deadline | April |
| Contact Name | High School Guidance Counselor or |
| Address | The Gary Educational Development Foundation 3757 W. 21st Ave. |
| State | IN |
| Zip Code | 46404 |
| Phone | 219 977-2192 |
| Fax | 219-977-6258 |
| E-mail | |
| Notes | |

| | |
|---|---|
| Type | School-Based |
| Major | All |
| Scholarship Name | Citizens Financial Services Scholarship |
| City | Gary |
| Organization | Indiana University Northwest |
| Amount | $1000 |
| Annual/One-Time | Annual |
| Requirements | The student must be a full-time, incoming freshman at IUN with outstanding high school records. The scholarship is renewable. |
| Deadline | See Financial Aid Director |
| Contact Name | Financial Aid Director |
| Address | Indiana University Northwest 3400 Broadway |
| State | IN |
| Zip Code | 46408 |
| Phone | 219-980-6777 |
| Fax | |
| E-mail | Klantz@iunhaw1.iun.indiana.edu |
| Notes | All students are encouraged to complete a free application for Federal Student Aid (FAFSA). Deadline is March 1. |

| | |
|---|---|
| Type | School-Based |
| Major | All |
| Scholarship Name | Community College of Indiana (Ivy Tech) |
| City | Gary |
| Organization | Community College of Indiana |
| Amount | Varies |
| Annual/One-Time | One Time |
| Requirements | For students with a score of 54 or higher on GED exam with recommendations and proof of extracurricular activities |
| Deadline | May 1 |
| Contact Name | Director of Financial Aid |
| Address | Community Colleges of Indiana 1440 E. 35th Ave. |
| State | IN |
| Zip Code | 46409 |
| Phone | 219-980-1111 |
| Fax | |
| E-mail | |
| Notes | All students are encouraged to complete a free application for Federal Student Aid (FAFSA). Deadline is March 1. |

| | |
|---|---|
| Type | School-Based |
| Major | All |
| Scholarship Name | Crown Point Community Foundation |
| City | Crown Point |
| Organization | Crown Point Community Foundation |
| Amount | $500 |
| Annual/One-Time | One Time |
| Requirements | Crown Point residents who attended fourth, fifth and sixth grade at Winfield Elementary School. |
| Deadline | April 1 |
| Contact Name | Crown Point Community Foundation |
| Address | P.O. Box 522 |
| State | IN |
| Zip Code | 46308-0522 |
| Phone | 219-662-7252 |
| Fax | 219-662-9493 |
| E-mail | cpcf@ursip.com |
| Notes | |

| | |
|---|---|
| Type | School-Based |
| Major | All |
| Scholarship Name | Elser, Don—Horace Mann Alumni Scholarship |
| City | Gary |
| Organization | Gary Educational Development Foundation |
| Amount | $800 |
| Annual/One-Time | One Time |
| Requirements | The graduating senior must be a student at Horace Mann High School in Gary. The student must obtain three written references of good character from "non-relatives", have an educational record of good attendance, have an identifiable post-secondary plan and a GPA between 2.0 and 3.5. |
| Deadline | April |
| Contact Name | High School Guidance Counselor or |
| Address | The Gary Educational Development Foundation 3757 W. 21st Ave. |
| State | IN |
| Zip Code | 46404 |
| Phone | 219-977-2192 |
| Fax | 219-977-6258 |
| E-mail | |
| Notes | |

| | |
|---|---|
| Type | School-Based |
| Major | All |
| Scholarship Name | Gary-Tuskegee Alumni Association |
| City | Gary |
| Organization | Gary Educational Development Foundation |
| Amount | $1000 |
| Annual/One-Time | One Time |
| Requirements | Two students will be selected. Students must be Gary high school students and plan a worthy career development at Tuskegee University. |
| Deadline | April |
| Contact Name | High School Guidance Counselor or |
| Address | Gary Educational Development Foundation<br>3757 W. 21st Ave. |
| State | IN |
| Zip Code | 46404 |
| Phone | 219-977-2192 |
| Fax | 219-977-6258 |
| E-mail | |
| Notes | |

| | |
|---|---|
| Type | School-Based |
| Major | All |
| Scholarship Name | Gyte, Millard E. and Christina A. Scholarship |
| City | Hammond |
| Organization | Purdue University Calumet |
| Amount | Contact Office of Financial |
| Annual/One-Time | One Time |
| Requirements | Student must have a 3.0 GPA, a combined SAT score of 1200 and top 10% of class. The student must also be enrolled in 6 hours of credits. |
| Deadline | March 1 |
| Contact Name | Office of Financial Aid |
| Address | Purdue Calumet Office 2200 169th Street |
| State | IN |
| Zip Code | 46323-2094 |
| Phone | 219-989-2301 |
| Fax | 219-989-2771 |
| E-mail | finaid@calumet.purdue.edu |
| Notes | Student needs to complete the Merit Scholarship application and a free application for Federal Student Aid (FAFSA). |

| | |
|---|---|
| Type | School-Based |
| Major | All |
| Scholarship Name | Hemminger, Susan Hay Scholarship Foundation |
| City | Michigan City |
| Organization | Hemminger Foundation |
| Amount | Up to $5,000 |
| Annual/One-Time | One Time |
| Requirements | Must be a LaPorte County high school graduate entering a four- or two-year college or university. Awarded on financial need, academic performance, service and leadership. Student must write a 500 word essay |
| Deadline | April 15 |
| Contact Name | Susan Hay Hemminger Scholarship Foundation |
| Address | P.O. Box 9242 |
| State | IN |
| Zip Code | 46360 |
| Phone | |
| Fax | |
| E-mail | |
| Notes | |

| | |
|---|---|
| Type | School-Based |
| Major | All |
| Scholarship Name | Husted, Robert G., M.D. Scholarship |
| City | Hammond |
| Organization | Purdue University Calumet |
| Amount | Contact Financial Aid Office |
| Annual/One-Time | One Time |
| Requirements | All levels of students are eligible for this scholarship. Students must have a GPA of 3.0 and enrolled in 12 credit hours. |
| Deadline | March |
| Contact Name | Office of Financial Aid |
| Address | Purdue University Calumet 2200 169th Street |
| State | IN |
| Zip Code | 46323-2094 |
| Phone | 219-989-2301 |
| Fax | 219-989-2771 |
| E-mail | finaid@calumet.purdue.edu |
| Notes | Merit Scholarship Application needed. |

| | |
|---|---|
| Type | School-Based |
| Major | All |
| Scholarship Name | Indiana University Alumni Loyalty Scholarship |
| City | Gary |
| Organization | Indiana University Northwest |
| Amount | $250 |
| Annual/One-Time | One Time |
| Requirements | The award is given to new full-time students who are nominated by an IUN alum and who meet certain criteria. |
| Deadline | Open |
| Contact Name | Director of Financial Aid |
| Address | Indiana University Northwest 3400 Broadway |
| State | IN |
| Zip Code | 46408 |
| Phone | 219-980-6777 |
| Fax | |
| E-mail | Klantz@iunhaw1.iun.indiana.edu |
| Notes | All students are encouraged to complete a free application for Federal Student Aid (FAFSA). Deadline is March 1. |

| | |
|---|---|
| Type | School-Based |
| Major | All |
| Scholarship Name | Indiana University Northwest GED Scholarship |
| City | Gary |
| Organization | Indiana University Northwest |
| Amount | See Financial Aid Director |
| Annual/One-Time | Annual |
| Requirements | The student must be a full-time freshman student who has a GED composite score of at least 64. Applicants must be at least 25 years of age and should have no prior college experience. The award is renewable if the recipient maintains a GPA of 3.33. |
| Deadline | See Financial Aid Director |
| Contact Name | Director of Financial Aid |
| Address | Indiana University Northwest 3400 Broadway |
| State | IN |
| Zip Code | 46408 |
| Phone | 219-980-6777 |
| Fax | |
| E-mail | Klantz@iunhaw1.iun.indiana.edu |
| Notes | All students are encouraged to complete a free application for Federal Student Aid (FAFSA). Deadline is March 1. |

| | |
|---|---|
| Type | School-Based |
| Major | All |
| Scholarship Name | Kabelin, Alice Scholarship |
| City | Michigan City |
| Organization | Unity Foundation of LaPorte County, Inc. |
| Amount | $1000 renewable |
| Annual/One-Time | Annual |
| Requirements | Graduates of LaPorte High School who are enrolled in an accredited college or university. Selection shall be based upon financial need, academic records, extracurricular activities and without regard to race, sex, religion, handicap and national origin. |
| Deadline | April 15 |
| Contact Name | Unity Foundation of LaPorte County, Inc. |
| Address | P.O. Box 527 |
| State | IN |
| Zip Code | 46361 |
| Phone | 219-879-0327 |
| Fax | |
| E-mail | Unity@NIIA.net |
| Notes | |

| | |
|---|---|
| Type | School-Based |
| Major | All |
| Scholarship Name | Kahn, Carl L. and David M. Scholarship |
| City | Gary |
| Organization | Indiana University Northwest |
| Amount | Full tuition |
| Annual/One-Time | One Time |
| Requirements | This scholarship is presented yearly to a student who graduates in the top 25 percent of his or her high school class and has an above average SAT score. |
| Deadline | Contact Financial Aid Director |
| Contact Name | Director of Financial Aid |
| Address | Indiana University Northwest 3400 Broadway |
| State | IN |
| Zip Code | 46408 |
| Phone | 219-980-6667 |
| Fax | |
| E-mail | Klantz@iunhaw1.iun.indiana.edu |
| Notes | All students are encouraged to complete a free application for Federal Student Aid (FAFSA). Deadline is March 1. |

| | |
|---|---|
| Type | School-Based |
| Major | All |
| Scholarship Name | Leek-Wesson, Barbara Scholarship |
| City | Gary |
| Organization | Gary Educational Development Foundation |
| Amount | $1000 |
| Annual/One-Time | One Time |
| Requirements | The graduating senior must be a student at Roosevelt High School or Martin Luther King Academy in Gary. The student must have a record of service to the school or community, exhibit positive attitude, has maintained average grades throughout high school and has a worthy career plan. |
| Deadline | April |
| Contact Name | High School Guidance Counselor or |
| Address | The Gary Educational Development Foundation 3757 W. 21st Ave. |
| State | IN |
| Zip Code | 46404 |
| Phone | 219-977-2192 |
| Fax | 219-977-6258 |
| E-mail | |
| Notes | |

| | |
|---|---|
| Type | School-Based |
| Major | All |
| Scholarship Name | **Lutheran High School Principal's Award** |
| City | Valparaiso |
| Organization | Valparaiso University |
| Amount | $500—$1000 |
| Annual/One-Time | Annual |
| Requirements | Entering Freshmen. Renewable with a GPA of 2.0 |
| Deadline | March 1 |
| Contact Name | High School Guidance Counselor or Director of Financial Aid |
| Address | Valparaiso University Kretzmann Hall |
| State | IN |
| Zip Code | 46383 |
| Phone | 219-464-5015 or |
| Fax | |
| E-mail | finaid@valpo.edu |
| Notes | All students are encouraged to complete a free application for Federal Student Aid (FAFSA). Deadline is March 1. |

| | |
|---|---|
| Type | School-Based |
| Major | All |
| Scholarship Name | **Lutheran Principal's Award** |
| City | Valparaiso |
| Organization | Valparaiso University |
| Amount | $500—$1500 |
| Annual/One-Time | Annual |
| Requirements | Must have graduated from a Lutheran high school. The award is based on academic achievement. Renewable with a 2.0 GPA. |
| Deadline | March 1 |
| Contact Name | Director of Financial Aid |
| Address | Valparaiso University Kretzmann Hall |
| State | IN |
| Zip Code | 46383 |
| Phone | 219-464-5015 or |
| Fax | |
| E-mail | finaid@valpo.edu |
| Notes | All students are encouraged to complete a free application for Federal Student Aid (FAFSA). Deadline is March 1. |

| | |
|---|---|
| Type | School-Based |
| Major | All |
| Scholarship Name | Minard, Manley Scholarship |
| City | Gary |
| Organization | Indiana University Northwest |
| Amount | $1000 |
| Annual/One-Time | One Time |
| Requirements | Awarded annually to a continuing student who has demonstrated outstanding academic achievement with a GPA of 3.5 or above who has attained junior or senior standing. |
| Deadline | Contact Financial Aid Director |
| Contact Name | Director of Financial Aid |
| Address | Indiana University Northwest 3400 Broadway |
| State | IN |
| Zip Code | 46408 |
| Phone | 219-980-6777 |
| Fax | |
| E-mail | Klantz@iunhaw1.iun.indiana.edu |
| Notes | All students are encouraged to complete a free application for Federal Student Aid (FAFSA). Deadline is March 1. |

| | |
|---|---|
| Type | School-Based |
| Major | All |
| Scholarship Name | National City Bank Scholarship |
| City | Gary |
| Organization | Indiana University Northwest |
| Amount | $500 |
| Annual/One-Time | Annual |
| Requirements | The award is renewable yearly for a full-time incoming Freshman of any age and in any field of study. |
| Deadline | Contact Financial Aid Director |
| Contact Name | Director of Financial Aid |
| Address | Indiana University Northwest 3400 Broadway |
| State | IN |
| Zip Code | 46408 |
| Phone | 219-980-6777 |
| Fax | |
| E-mail | Klantz@iunhaw1.iun.indiana.edu |
| Notes | All students are encouraged to complete a free application for Federal Student Aid (FAFSA). Deadline is March 1. |

| | |
|---|---|
| Type | School-Based |
| Major | All |
| Scholarship Name | Omega Psi Phi Fraternity |
| City | Gary |
| Organization | Gary Educational Development Foundation |
| Amount | $1000 |
| Annual/One-Time | One Time |
| Requirements | The graduating senior must be a minority male student at a Gary high school. The student must have a record of satisfactory or better scholastic achievements, a record of good citizenship and positive community involvement, display high character and leadership qualities. |
| Deadline | April |
| Contact Name | High School Guidance Counselor or |
| Address | The Gary Educational Development Foundation 3757 W. 21st Ave. |
| State | IN |
| Zip Code | 46404 |
| Phone | 219-977-2192 |
| Fax | 219-977-6258 |
| E-mail | |
| Notes | |

| | |
|---|---|
| Type | School-Based |
| Major | All |
| Scholarship Name | PAAC Phone A Thon Scholarship |
| City | Hammond |
| Organization | Purdue University Calumet |
| Amount | Contact Financial Aid Office |
| Annual/One-Time | One Time |
| Requirements | Student must be top 10% of class with a combined SAT of 1200 and a GPA of 3.0. This scholarship is for all levels. |
| Deadline | March |
| Contact Name | Office of Financial Aid |
| Address | Purdue University Calumet 2200 169th Street |
| State | IN |
| Zip Code | 46323-2094 |
| Phone | 219-989-2301 |
| Fax | 219-989-2771 |
| E-mail | finaid@calumet.purdue.edu |
| Notes | Merit Scholarship Application must be completed. |

| | |
|---|---|
| Type | School-Based |
| Major | All |
| Scholarship Name | Plucinski, Edward & Marie Scholarship |
| City | Hammond |
| Organization | Purdue University Calumet |
| Amount | Contact Office of Financial Aid |
| Annual/One-Time | One Time |
| Requirements | Student must have a GPA of 3.0. |
| Deadline | March 1 |
| Contact Name | Office of Financial Aid |
| Address | Purdue University Calumet 2200 169th Street |
| State | IN |
| Zip Code | 46323-2094 |
| Phone | 219-989-2301 |
| Fax | 219-989-2771 |
| E-mail | finaid@calumet.purdue.edu |
| Notes | Merit Scholarship Application required. |

| | |
|---|---|
| Type | School-Based |
| Major | All |
| Scholarship Name | Powers, Donald S. Athletic Scholarship |
| City | Hammond |
| Organization | Purdue University Calumet |
| Amount | Contact Director of Financial Aid |
| Annual/One-Time | One Time |
| Requirements | Recipient should be in the University Athletics Program. The Director of Athletics selects candidates and committee selects winners. |
| Deadline | March 1 |
| Contact Name | Office of Financial Aid |
| Address | Purdue University Calumet 2200 169th Street |
| State | IN |
| Zip Code | 46323-2094 |
| Phone | 219-989-2301 |
| Fax | 219-989-2771 |
| E-mail | finaid@calumet.purdue.edu |
| Notes | All students are encouraged to complete a free application for Federal Student Aid (FAFSA). Deadline is March 1. |

| | |
|---|---|
| Type | School-Based |
| Major | All |
| Scholarship Name | Purdue North Central Scholarships for High School Students |
| City | Westville |
| Organization | Purdue North Central |
| Amount | Up to $1000 |
| Annual/One-Time | One Time |
| Requirements | The student must have a minimum high school GPA of 3.0, a minimum SAT of 1000 or ACT of 21 and enroll for at least 12 credit hours at PU/NC each semester during the school year. |
| Deadline | Contact Financial Aid Director |
| Contact Name | Director of Financial Aid |
| Address | Purdue North Central 1401 S. U.S. 421 |
| State | IN |
| Zip Code | 46391-9542 |
| Phone | 219-872-0527 xt. 5505 |
| Fax | |
| E-mail | |
| Notes | All students are encouraged to complete a free application for Federal Student Aid (FAFSA). Deadline is March 1. |

| | |
|---|---|
| Type | School-Based |
| Major | All |
| Scholarship Name | Rocke, Robert A. and Dorothy W. Scholarship |
| City | Michigan City |
| Organization | Unity Foundation |
| Amount | $1000 |
| Annual/One-Time | Annual |
| Requirements | Graduates of LaPorte High School who are enrolled in an accredited college or university. Selection shall be based on need and demonstrated desire to succeed in the recipient's chosen field. |
| Deadline | April |
| Contact Name | Unity foundation of LaPorte County, Inc. |
| Address | P.O. Box 527 |
| State | IN |
| Zip Code | 46361 |
| Phone | 219-879-0327 |
| Fax | |
| E-mail | |
| Notes | All students are encouraged to complete a free application for Federal Student Aid (FAFSA). Deadline is March 1. |

| | |
|---|---|
| Type | School-Based |
| Major | All |
| Scholarship Name | **Roosevelt High School Alumni Association** |
| City | Gary |
| Organization | Gary Educational Development Foundation |
| Amount | $700 |
| Annual/One-Time | One Time |
| Requirements | The graduating senior must be a student at Gary Roosevelt High School. The student must have a high standing in honor, scholarship and community service. The student must provide references and provide an outline of a post-secondary education plan. |
| Deadline | April |
| Contact Name | High School Guidance Counselor or |
| Address | The Gary Educational Development Foundation 3757 W. 21st Ave. |
| State | IN |
| Zip Code | 46404 |
| Phone | 219-977-2192 |
| Fax | 219-977-6258 |
| E-mail | |
| Notes | |

| | |
|---|---|
| Type | School-Based |
| Major | All |
| Scholarship Name | Rotary 2001—2002 Foundation Ambassadorial Scholarship |
| City | Hammond |
| Organization | Rotary Foundation |
| Amount | $12,000—$25,000 |
| Annual/One-Time | One Time |
| Requirements | Must complete a 2001—2002 Ambassadorial Scholarship Application. |
| Deadline | April |
| Contact Name | James V. Donovan, President |
| Address | Tri-Electronics 6231 Calumet |
| State | IN |
| Zip Code | 46323-4310 |
| Phone | 219-931-6850 |
| Fax | 219-933-3545 |
| E-mail | finaid@calumet.purdue.edu |
| Notes | |

| | |
|---|---|
| **Type** | School-Based |
| **Major** | All |
| **Scholarship Name** | Rotary Golden Anniversary Scholarship |
| **City** | Hammond |
| **Organization** | Purdue University Calumet |
| **Amount** | Contact Director of Financial Aid |
| **Annual/One-Time** | One Time |
| **Requirements** | For undergraduate students with a 2.0 GPA and enrolled with 6 hours. |
| **Deadline** | March |
| **Contact Name** | Office of Financial Aid |
| **Address** | Purdue University Calumet 2200 169th Street |
| **State** | IN |
| **Zip Code** | 46323-2094 |
| **Phone** | 219-989-2301 |
| **Fax** | 219-989-2772 |
| **E-mail** | finaid@calumet.purdue.edu |
| **Notes** | Student must complete a Free Application for Federal Student Aid (FAFSA) and the Merit Scholarship Application. |

| | |
|---|---|
| Type | School-Based |
| Major | All |
| Scholarship Name | Shawn Moyer Memorial Scholarship |
| City | Valparaiso |
| Organization | Porter County Community Foundation |
| Amount | Contact Foundation |
| Annual/One-Time | One Time |
| Requirements | The student must be a Kouts High School graduate attending a four-year college or university in Indiana. Preference will be given to students who elect to attend a Christian institution. |
| Deadline | Contact Foundation |
| Contact Name | Barbara A. Young |
| Address | Porter County Community Foundation P.O. Box 302 |
| State | IN |
| Zip Code | 46384 |
| Phone | 219-465-0294 |
| Fax | |
| E-mail | |
| Notes | |

| | |
|---|---|
| Type | School-Based |
| Major | All |
| Scholarship Name | Society of Hispanic Professional Engineers |
| City | Hammond |
| Organization | Society of Hispanic Professional Engineers |
| Amount | Open |
| Annual/One-Time | One Time |
| Requirements | Minimum 2.5 GPA and will attend Purdue Calumet. |
| Deadline | April |
| Contact Name | Society of Hispanic Professional Engineers |
| Address | Purdue University Calumet 2200 169th Street |
| State | IN |
| Zip Code | 46323 |
| Phone | 219-989-2301 |
| Fax | 219-989-2771 |
| E-mail | |
| Notes | |

| | |
|---|---|
| Type | School-Based |
| Major | All |
| Scholarship Name | Superintendent's Rotating Scholarship |
| City | Gary |
| Organization | Gary Educational Development Foundation |
| Amount | $1000 |
| Annual/One-Time | One Time |
| Requirements | Awarded to one student at all Gary high schools on a rotating basis. The graduating seniors must possess a GPA between 2.0 and 2.9 and have an educational plan. |
| Deadline | April |
| Contact Name | High School Guidance Counselor or |
| Address | Gary Educational Development Foundation<br>3757 W. 21st. Ave. |
| State | IN |
| Zip Code | 46404 |
| Phone | 219-977-2192 |
| Fax | 219-977-6258 |
| E-mail | |
| Notes | |

| | |
|---|---|
| Type | School-Based |
| Major | All |
| Scholarship Name | Tatum, H. Theo Scholarship |
| City | Gary |
| Organization | Gary Educational Development Foundation |
| Amount | $1200 |
| Annual/One-Time | One Time |
| Requirements | The graduating senior must be a student at Gary Roosevelt High School. The recipient must show exemplary scholastic achievement, possess high qualities of leadership and character, a record of service to the school and/or community, provide references and have a post-secondary education plan. |
| Deadline | April |
| Contact Name | High School Guidance Counselor or |
| Address | The Gary Educational Development Foundation 3757 W. 21st Ave. |
| State | IN |
| Zip Code | 46404 |
| Phone | 219-977-2192 |
| Fax | 219-977-6258 |
| E-mail | |
| Notes | |

| | |
|---|---|
| Type | School-Based |
| Major | All |
| Scholarship Name | Taylor, Jack L. Scholarship |
| City | Indianapolis |
| Organization | Jack L. Taylor Scholarship |
| Amount | Contact Scholarship |
| Annual/One-Time | One Time |
| Requirements | Scholarship awarded to graduates of Whiting High School. |
| Deadline | Contact Scholarship Fund |
| Contact Name | Gail Randall |
| Address | Jack L. Taylor Scholarship c/o Bank One Trust Group<br>111 Monument Circle |
| State | IN |
| Zip Code | 46277-0115 |
| Phone | |
| Fax | |
| E-mail | |
| Notes | |

| | |
|---|---|
| Type | School-Based |
| Major | All |
| Scholarship Name | Williams, David Scholarship |
| City | Gary |
| Organization | Gary Educational Development Foundation |
| Amount | $800 |
| Annual/One-Time | One Time |
| Requirements | This award is given to a graduating senior from Roosevelt High School in Gary. The student must be pursuing a post-secondary education in preparation for a technical or professional career. |
| Deadline | April |
| Contact Name | High School Guidance Counselor or |
| Address | The Gary Educational Development Foundation 3757 W. 21st. Ave. |
| State | IN |
| Zip Code | 46404 |
| Phone | 219-977-2192 |
| Fax | 219-977-6258 |
| E-mail | |
| Notes | |

| | |
|---|---|
| Type | School-Based |
| Major | All |
| Scholarship Name | Wirt, William A. Scholarship |
| City | Gary |
| Organization | Gary Educational Development Foundation |
| Amount | $800 |
| Annual/One-Time | One Time |
| Requirements | The graduating senior must be a student at William A. Wirt High School in Gary. The student must have exemplary scholarship achievement —2.75 GPA or better, have an appropriate education plan, have a positive record of service to the school and/or community and be a good citizen. |
| Deadline | April |
| Contact Name | High School Guidance Counselor or |
| Address | The Gary Educational Development Foundation 3757 W. 21st Ave. |
| State | IN |
| Zip Code | 46404 |
| Phone | 219-977-2192 |
| Fax | 219-977-6258 |
| E-mail | |
| Notes | |

| | |
|---|---|
| Type | School-Based |
| Major | Art or History |
| Scholarship Name | Mohamed, John Scholarship |
| City | Hammond |
| Organization | Purdue Calumet University |
| Amount | Contact Financial Aid Office |
| Annual/One-Time | One Time |
| Requirements | The student should have a GPA of 3.0 and enrolled in 12 credit hours. |
| Deadline | March 1 |
| Contact Name | Office of Financial Aid |
| Address | Purdue University Calumet 2200 169th Street |
| State | IN |
| Zip Code | 46232-2094 |
| Phone | 219-989-2301 |
| Fax | 219-989-2771 |
| E-mail | finaid@calumet.purdue.edu |
| Notes | Student needs to complete the Merit Scholarship application and a free application for Federal Student Aid (FAFSA). |

| | |
|---|---|
| Type | School-Based |
| Major | Banking, Business or Education |
| Scholarship Name | Knox, Joseph Scholarship |
| City | Gary |
| Organization | Gary Educational Development Foundation |
| Amount | $700 to each school |
| Annual/One-Time | One Time |
| Requirements | The graduating senior must be a student at one of the six Gary high schools or the Gary Area Career Center. Student must enroll at a university, demonstrate positive personal qualities, have a GPA of 2.0 or better and have a positive high school experience. The student must maintain a GPA of 2.0 for the duration of the scholarship. |
| Deadline | April |
| Contact Name | High School Guidance Counselor or |
| Address | The Gary Educational Development Foundation 3757 W. 21st Ave. |
| State | IN |
| Zip Code | 46404 |
| Phone | 219-977-2192 |
| Fax | 219-977-6258 |
| E-mail | |
| Notes | |

| | |
|---|---|
| Type | School-Based |
| Major | Education |
| Scholarship Name | Jones, Robert E. Scholarship |
| City | Gary |
| Organization | Gary Educational Development Foundation |
| Amount | $1000 |
| Annual/One-Time | One Time |
| Requirements | The graduating senior must be a student at Roosevelt Highs School. The student must have a "C" or better average, displays positive leadership, have positive personal qualities observed directly or indirectly, a good record of service to school and/or community and a career plan. |
| Deadline | April |
| Contact Name | High School Guidance Counselor or |
| Address | The Gary Educational Development Foundation 3757 W. 21st Ave. |
| State | IN |
| Zip Code | 46404 |
| Phone | 219-977-2192 |
| Fax | 219-977-6258 |
| E-mail | |
| Notes | |

| | |
|---|---|
| Type | School-Based |
| Major | Elementary Ed, History, Political Science |
| Scholarship Name | Withers Scholars Foundation |
| City | Fort Wayne |
| Organization | Withers Scholars Foundation |
| Amount | $600—$2000 |
| Annual/One-Time | Annual |
| Requirements | Must be a junior or senior attending IUPUI at Fort Wayne. |
| Deadline | Open |
| Contact Name | Withers Scholars Foundation |
| Address | Office of Financial Aid Kettler Hall, IUPUI |
| State | IN |
| Zip Code | 46805 |
| Phone | |
| Fax | |
| E-mail | |
| Notes | |

| | |
|---|---|
| Type | School-Based |
| Major | Environmental Science, Business, Health |
| Scholarship Name | Northwest Indiana Water Company Scholarship |
| City | Gary |
| Organization | Indiana University Northwest |
| Amount | |
| Annual/One-Time | One Time |
| Requirements | The scholarship is awarded to a full-time student who holds junior standing with a GPA of 3.0 or better. Preference is given to a student who is a resident of Lake or Porter County. |
| Deadline | Contact Director of Financial |
| Contact Name | Director of Financial Aid |
| Address | Indiana University Northwest 3400 Broadway |
| State | IN |
| Zip Code | 46408 |
| Phone | 219-980-6777 |
| Fax | |
| E-mail | Klantz@iunhaw1.iun.indiana.edu |
| Notes | All students are encouraged to complete a free application for Federal Student Aid (FAFSA). Deadline is March 1. |

| | |
|---|---|
| Type | School-Based |
| Major | Health related |
| Scholarship Name | Ferus, Rosemary Sister Memorial Scholarship |
| City | Hammond |
| Organization | Purdue University Calumet |
| Amount | Contact Financial Aid Office |
| Annual/One-Time | One Time |
| Requirements | Recipient must be in a healthcare-related field, have a GPA of 3.0 and enrolled in 9 credit hours. All levels of students may apply. |
| Deadline | |
| Contact Name | Office of Financial Aid |
| Address | Purdue University Calumet 2200 169th Street |
| State | IN |
| Zip Code | 46323-2094 |
| Phone | 219-989-2301 |
| Fax | 219-989-2771 |
| E-mail | finaid@calumet.purdue.edu |
| Notes | Student should also complete a Free Application for Federal Student Aid (FAFSA) and a Purdue Calumet Merit Scholarship Application. |

| | |
|---|---|
| Type | School-Based |
| Major | Mathematics/Physics/Chemistry |
| Scholarship Name | Forbes, Jack Memorial Scholarship |
| City | Hammond |
| Organization | Purdue University Calumet |
| Amount | Contact Office of Financial Aid |
| Annual/One-Time | One Time |
| Requirements | The student must be in the top 25% of his/her class, have a combined SAT of 1100, and a GPA of 3.0 and enrolled in 9 hours. This award is for undergraduates of all levels. |
| Deadline | March |
| Contact Name | Office of Financial Aid |
| Address | Purdue University Calumet 2200 169th Street |
| State | IN |
| Zip Code | 46323-2094 |
| Phone | 219-989-2301 |
| Fax | 219-989-2771 |
| E-mail | finaid@calumet.purdue.edu |
| Notes | Merit Scholarship Application required. |

| | |
|---|---|
| Type | School-Based |
| Major | Medicine |
| Scholarship Name | Indiana University Northwest |
| City | Gary |
| Organization | Indiana University Northwest |
| Amount | full-tuition (eight years) |
| Annual/One-Time | Annual |
| Requirements | The scholarships is offered to students from urban areas who want to practice medicine as a profession. The scholarship is for the completion of an undergraduate degree at IU School of Medicine. |
| Deadline | April 1 |
| Contact Name | Dr. Tuncay/Dr. Baldwin |
| Address | Indiana University Northwest<br>3400 Broadway |
| State | IN |
| Zip Code | 46408 |
| Phone | 219-980-6745/219-980-6555 |
| Fax | |
| E-mail | |
| Notes | |

| | |
|---|---|
| Type | School-Based |
| Major | Nursing |
| Scholarship Name | **Purdue University Alumni & Friends of Graduate Nursing** |
| City | Hammond |
| Organization | Purdue University Calumet |
| Amount | varies |
| Annual/One-Time | One Time |
| Requirements | Graduate student in nursing at Purdue Calumet. |
| Deadline | March 1 |
| Contact Name | Office of Financial Aid |
| Address | Purdue University of Calumet 2200 169th Street |
| State | IN |
| Zip Code | 46323-2094 |
| Phone | 219-989-2301 |
| Fax | 219-989-2771 |
| E-mail | finaid@calumet.purdue.edu |
| Notes | All students are encouraged to complete a free application for Federal Student Aid (FAFSA). Deadline is March 1. |

| | |
|---|---|
| Type | School-Based |
| Major | Nursing |
| Scholarship Name | Purdue University Calumet Alumni & Friends of B.S. Nursing |
| City | Hammond |
| Organization | Purdue University Calumet |
| Amount | See Financial Aid Director |
| Annual/One-Time | One Time |
| Requirements | Senior student in nursing with a GPA of 3.5. |
| Deadline | March 1 |
| Contact Name | Office of Financial Aid |
| Address | Purdue University Calumet 2200 169th Street |
| State | IN |
| Zip Code | 46323-2094 |
| Phone | 219-989-2301 |
| Fax | 219-989-2771 |
| E-mail | finaid@calumet.purdue.edu |
| Notes | All students are encouraged to complete a free application for Federal Student Aid (FAFSA). Deadline is March 1. |

| | |
|---|---|
| Type | School-Based |
| Major | Nursing |
| Scholarship Name | Riley, Charlotte Nursing Scholarship |
| City | Hammond |
| Organization | Purdue University Calumet School of |
| Amount | Contact School of Nursing |
| Annual/One-Time | One Time |
| Requirements | The Purdue Calumet Nursing Department identifies a recipient of this scholarship. Applicant must be interested in HOSPICE. |
| Deadline | Contact School of Nursing |
| Contact Name | School of Nursing |
| Address | Purdue University Calumet
2200 169th Street |
| State | IN |
| Zip Code | 46323 |
| Phone | 219-989-2818 |
| Fax | |
| E-mail | finaid@calumet.purdue.edu |
| Notes | Purdue Calumet Merit Scholarship Application preferred, but not required. |

| | |
|---|---|
| Type | School-Based |
| Major | Science or Nursing |
| Scholarship Name | Science and Nursing Memorial Talent Award |
| City | Gary |
| Organization | Purdue University Calumet |
| Amount | Contact Financial Aid Office |
| Annual/One-Time | One Time |
| Requirements | The student must be in the top 10% of his/her class with a combined SAT of 1200 and a GPA of 3.0. The student must be enrolled in 12 credit hours. All levels of students may apply. |
| Deadline | March |
| Contact Name | Office of Financial Aid |
| Address | Purdue University Calumet 2200 169th Street |
| State | IN |
| Zip Code | 46323-2094 |
| Phone | 219-989-2301 |
| Fax | 219-989-2771 |
| E-mail | finaid@calumet.purdue.edu |
| Notes | Student must complete a Merit Scholarship Application. |

| | |
|---|---|
| Type | School-Based |
| Major | Science related |
| Scholarship Name | Matthews, Joseph Scholarship |
| City | Gary |
| Organization | Gary Educational Development Foundation |
| Amount | $800 |
| Annual/One-Time | One Time |
| Requirements | The graduating senior must be a student at Gary Roosevelt High School. The student must display exemplary scholastic achievement with a GPA of 3.0 or better, high qualities of leadership and character, possess at least one letter in a high school team sport, provide references, and have a post-secondary education plan. |
| Deadline | April |
| Contact Name | High School Guidance Counselor or |
| Address | The Gary Educational Development Foundation 3757 W. 21st Ave. |
| State | IN |
| Zip Code | 46404 |
| Phone | 219-977-2192 |
| Fax | 219-977-6258 |
| E-mail | |
| Notes | |

| | |
|---|---|
| Type | School-Based |
| Major | Technology |
| Scholarship Name | School or Tech Class of '67 Scholarship |
| City | Hammond |
| Organization | Purdue University Calumet |
| Amount | Contact Financial Aid Office |
| Annual/One-Time | One Time |
| Requirements | The student must be in the top 10% of his/her class with a combined SAT of 1200 and a GPA of 2.5. Student must also be enrolled in 6 credit hours. This scholarship is for all levels. |
| Deadline | March |
| Contact Name | Office of Financial Aid |
| Address | Purdue University Calumet 2200 169th Street |
| State | IN |
| Zip Code | 46323-2094 |
| Phone | 219-989-2301 |
| Fax | 219-989-2771 |
| E-mail | finaid@calumet.purdue.edu |
| Notes | Must complete a Merit Scholarship Application. |

# VOCATIONAL SCHOLARSHIPS

| | |
|---|---|
| Type | Vocational |
| Major | Art related field |
| Scholarship Name | Northern Indiana Arts Association |
| City | Munster |
| Organization | Northern Indiana Arts Association |
| Amount | $5000 |
| Annual/One-Time | One Time |
| Requirements | Students must be a junior or senior in high school planning to major in an art related field. Student must also supply an art portfolio. |
| Deadline | May 1 |
| Contact Name | High School Art Teacher or |
| Address | Northern Indiana Arts Association Center For Performing Arts |
| State | IN |
| Zip Code | 46321 |
| Phone | 219-836-1839 |
| Fax | |
| E-mail | |
| Notes | |

| | |
|---|---|
| Type | Vocational |
| Major | Biology |
| Scholarship Name | Botany Award |
| City | Hammond |
| Organization | Purdue University Calumet |
| Amount | Contact Director of Financial Aid |
| Annual/One-Time | One Time |
| Requirements | Must be a male or female with a GPA of 3.0 attending PUC with 6 hours or more. |
| Deadline | March 1 |
| Contact Name | Office of Financial Aid |
| Address | Purdue University Calumet 2200 169th Street |
| State | IN |
| Zip Code | 46323-2094 |
| Phone | 219-989-2301 |
| Fax | 219-989-2771 |
| E-mail | finaid@calumet.purdue.edu |
| Notes | Student should also complete the Purdue Calumet Merit Scholarship Application. |

| | |
|---|---|
| Type | Vocational |
| Major | Business |
| Scholarship Name | Dudzik, Wanda Memorial Scholarship |
| City | Gary |
| Organization | Indiana University Northwest |
| Amount | $30,000 divided among 23 students |
| Annual/One-Time | One Time |
| Requirements | The students must be a major in the Division of Business and Economics. |
| Deadline | See Financial Aid Director |
| Contact Name | Director of Financial Aid |
| Address | Indiana University Northwest 3400 Broadway |
| State | IN |
| Zip Code | 46408 |
| Phone | 219-980-6777 |
| Fax | |
| E-mail | Klantz@iunhaw1.iun.indiana.edu |
| Notes | All students are encouraged to complete a free application for Federal Student Aid (FAFSA). Deadline is March 1. |

| | |
|---|---|
| Type | Vocational |
| Major | Business, Economics and RHI |
| Scholarship Name | Dudzik, Wanda Memorial Scholarship |
| City | Hammond |
| Organization | Purdue University Calumet |
| Amount | Contact Director of Financial Aid |
| Annual/One-Time | One Time |
| Requirements | Students must have a GPA of 3.0 and a combined SAT of 900. RHI students must complete a Merit Scholarship Application. Business & Economics Management students must complete a Management Scholarship Application. All level of students may apply. |
| Deadline | March |
| Contact Name | Office of Financial Aid |
| Address | Purdue University Calumet 2200 169th Street |
| State | IN |
| Zip Code | 46323-2094 |
| Phone | 219-989-2301 |
| Fax | 219-989-2771 |
| E-mail | finaid@calumet.purdue.edu |
| Notes | |

| | |
|---|---|
| Type | Vocational |
| Major | Chemistry |
| Scholarship Name | Chemistry Merit Scholarship |
| City | Hammond |
| Organization | Purdue University Calumet |
| Amount | Contact Director of Financial Aid |
| Annual/One-Time | One Time |
| Requirements | The student must have a GPA of 2.5 and be enrolled in at least 12 hours. |
| Deadline | March 1 |
| Contact Name | Office of Financial Aid |
| Address | Purdue University Calumet 2200 169th Street |
| State | IN |
| Zip Code | 46323-2094 |
| Phone | 219-989-2301 |
| Fax | 219-989-2771 |
| E-mail | finaid@calumet.purdue.edu |
| Notes | Student should also complete the Purdue Calumet Merit Scholarship Application. |

| | |
|---|---|
| Type | Vocational |
| Major | Chemistry |
| Scholarship Name | Dow Scholarship |
| City | Valparaiso |
| Organization | Valparaiso University |
| Amount | $2500 |
| Annual/One-Time | Annual |
| Requirements | Freshmen entering Valparaiso University who intend to pursue a doctorate in chemistry. The award is renewable with a 3.0 GPA. |
| Deadline | March 1 |
| Contact Name | Director of Financial Aid |
| Address | Valparaiso University Kretzmann Hall |
| State | IN |
| Zip Code | 46383 |
| Phone | 219-464-5015 or |
| Fax | |
| E-mail | finaid@valpo.edu |
| Notes | All students are encouraged to complete a free application for Federal Student Aid (FAFSA). Deadline is March 1. |

*Karen L. Williams*

| | |
|---|---|
| **Type** | Vocational |
| **Major** | Communications |
| **Scholarship Name** | JLR Memorial Scholarship |
| **City** | Hammond |
| **Organization** | Purdue University Calumet |
| **Amount** | Contact Financial Aid |
| **Annual/One-Time** | One Time |
| **Requirements** | Student must have a combined SAT score of 1200, a GPA of 3.0 and be in the top 10% of his/her class. |
| **Deadline** | March 1 |
| **Contact Name** | Office of Financial Aid |
| **Address** | Purdue University Calumet 2200 169th Street |
| **State** | IN |
| **Zip Code** | 46323-2094 |
| **Phone** | 219-989-2301 |
| **Fax** | 219-989-2771 |
| **E-mail** | finaid@calumet.purdue.edu |
| **Notes** | Students must complete a Merit Scholarship application. |

| | |
|---|---|
| Major | Vocational Communications and/or Engineering |
| Scholarship Name | Great Lakes Broadcasting |
| City | Gary |
| Organization | Gary Educational Development Foundation |
| Amount | $1000 |
| Annual/One-Time | One Time |
| Requirements | Applicant must pursue a career in the field of communications and/or engineering and have a GPA of 2.5 or better. |
| Deadline | April |
| Contact Name | High School Guidance Counselor of |
| Address | Gary Educational Development Foundation 3757 W. 21st Avenue |
| State | IN |
| Zip Code | 46404-2899 |
| Phone | 219-977-2191 |
| Fax | 219-977-6258 |
| E-mail | |
| Notes | |

| | |
|---|---|
| Type | Vocational |
| Major | Dentistry |
| Scholarship Name | Chirila, Romy S. Scholarship |
| City | Gary |
| Organization | Indiana University Northwest |
| Amount | See Financial Aid Director |
| Annual/One-Time | One Time |
| Requirements | The student must plan to attend IUN and have a GPA of 3.0 and an interest in Dentistry. |
| Deadline | See Financial Aid Director |
| Contact Name | Director of Financial Aid |
| Address | Indiana University Northwest 3400 Broadway |
| State | IN |
| Zip Code | 46408 |
| Phone | 219-980-6777 |
| Fax | |
| E-mail | Klantz@iunhaw1.iun.indiana.edu |
| Notes | All students are encouraged to complete a free application for Federal Student Aid (FAFSA). Deadline is March 1. |

| | |
|---|---|
| Type | Vocational |
| Major | Electrical Engineering Technology |
| Scholarship Name | Miller, Charles E. Memorial Scholarship |
| City | Hammond |
| Organization | Purdue University Calumet |
| Amount | Contact Financial Aid Director |
| Annual/One-Time | One Time |
| Requirements | Undergraduate awardees selected by EET faculty in conjunction with the Office of Financial Aid. Student should also complete the Purdue Calumet Merit Scholarship Application. Student should have a combined SAT of 1200 and a GPA of 2.50 and in the top 25% of their class. |
| Deadline | March 1 |
| Contact Name | Office of Financial Aid |
| Address | Purdue University Calumet 2200 169th Street |
| State | IN |
| Zip Code | 46323-2094 |
| Phone | 219-989-2301 |
| Fax | 219-989-2771 |
| E-mail | finaid@calumet.purdue.edu |
| Notes | All students are encouraged to complete a free application for Federal Student Aid (FAFSA). Deadline is March 1. |

| | |
|---|---|
| Type | Vocational |
| Major | Elementary Education |
| Scholarship Name | Dawson, Carrie B. Scholarship |
| City | Gary |
| Organization | The Gary Educational Development Foundation |
| Amount | $800 |
| Annual/One-Time | One Time |
| Requirements | The graduating senior must be a student at a Gary high school and has displayed outstanding scholastic achievements, scholastic aptitude and/or major leadership qualities, has demonstrated high qualities of character and citizenship. |
| Deadline | April |
| Contact Name | High School Guidance Counselor or |
| Address | The Gary Educational Development Foundation 3757 W. 21st Ave. |
| State | IN |
| Zip Code | 46404 |
| Phone | 219 977-2192 |
| Fax | 219-977-6258 |
| E-mail | |
| Notes | |

| | |
|---|---|
| Type | Vocational |
| Major | Engineering |
| Scholarship Name | Smith, Sydney Memorial Endowed Scholarship |
| City | Hammond |
| Organization | Purdue University Calumet |
| Amount | Contact Financial Aid Office |
| Annual/One-Time | One Time |
| Requirements | Student must be in top 25% of the class with a combined SAT score of 1200, a GPA of 2.5 with 6 credit hours. All levels of students may apply. |
| Deadline | March |
| Contact Name | Office of Financial Aid |
| Address | Purdue University Calumet 2200 169th Street |
| State | IN |
| Zip Code | 46323-2094 |
| Phone | 219-989-2301 |
| Fax | 219-989-2771 |
| E-mail | finaid@calumet.purdue.edu |
| Notes | Students must complete a Free Application for Federal Student Aid (FAFSA) and the Merit Scholarship Application. |

| | |
|---|---|
| Type | Vocational |
| Major | Engineering |
| Scholarship Name | Smith, Sydney Merit Award |
| City | Hammond |
| Organization | Purdue University Calumet |
| Amount | Contact Financial Aid Office |
| Annual/One-Time | One Time |
| Requirements | Available to all levels of students in the top 25% of their class, combined SAT of 1200, GPA 2.5 and enrolled in at least 6 hours. |
| Deadline | March |
| Contact Name | Office of Financial Aid |
| Address | Purdue University Calumet 2200 169th Street |
| State | IN |
| Zip Code | 46323-2094 |
| Phone | 219-989-2301 |
| Fax | 219-989-2771 |
| E-mail | finaid@calumet.purdue.edu |
| Notes | Student must complete a Merit Scholarship Application. |

| | |
|---|---|
| Type | Vocational |
| Major | Engineering/Electrical Engineering Tech. |
| Scholarship Name | DiVincent, Tony Award |
| City | Hammond |
| Organization | Purdue Calumet University |
| Amount | Contact Financial Aid Office |
| Annual/One-Time | One Time |
| Requirements | For junior or senior college students with a 2.80 GPA and enrolled in 12 hours of study. They must have an interest in acoustical engineering and/or consumer electronics. |
| Deadline | March |
| Contact Name | Office of Financial Aid |
| Address | Purdue University Calumet 2200 169th Street |
| State | IN |
| Zip Code | 46323-2094 |
| Phone | 219-989-2301 |
| Fax | 219-989-2771 |
| E-mail | finaid@calumet.purdue.edu |
| Notes | Students must complete a Merit Scholarship Application. |

| | |
|---|---|
| Type | Vocational |
| Major | Engineering/Management/Technology |
| Scholarship Name | Taylor, E. Winthrop Memorial Scholarship |
| City | Hammond |
| Organization | Purdue University Calumet |
| Amount | Contact Director of Financial Aid |
| Annual/One-Time | One Time |
| Requirements | Student must be a freshman with a 1200 combined SAT score, GPA of 3.0 and be in the top 10% of his/her class. |
| Deadline | March 1 |
| Contact Name | Office of Financial Aid |
| Address | Purdue University Calumet 2200 169th Street |
| State | IN |
| Zip Code | 46323-2094 |
| Phone | 219-989-2301 |
| Fax | 219-989-2771 |
| E-mail | finaid@calumet.purdue.edu |
| Notes | |

| | |
|---|---|
| Type | Vocational |
| Major | Environmental Studies |
| Scholarship Name | Air & Waste Management Association Scholarship |
| City | Hammond |
| Organization | Purdue University Calumet |
| Amount | See Financial Aid Director |
| Annual/One-Time | One Time |
| Requirements | Students must be a senior or above and have a 3.0 GPA, enrolled in 12 hours. |
| Deadline | February |
| Contact Name | Office of Financial Aid |
| Address | Purdue University Calumet 2200 169th Street |
| State | IN |
| Zip Code | 46323-2094 |
| Phone | 219-989-2301 |
| Fax | 219-989-2771 |
| E-mail | finaid@calumet.purdue.edu |
| Notes | All students are encouraged to complete a free application for Federal Student Aid (FAFSA). Deadline is March 1. |

| | |
|---|---|
| Type | Vocational |
| Major | Foreign service |
| Scholarship Name | Angus Ward Foreign Service Scholarship |
| City | Valparaiso |
| Organization | Valparaiso University |
| Amount | $1000 (renewable) |
| Annual/One-Time | Annual |
| Requirements | An entering freshman at Valparaiso University pursuing a career in the U.S. Foreign Service. The award is based on academic achievement and financial need. Renewable with a 2.0 GPA. |
| Deadline | March 1 |
| Contact Name | Director of Financial Aid |
| Address | Kretzmann Hall<br>Valparaiso University |
| State | IN |
| Zip Code | 46383 |
| Phone | 219-464-5015 or |
| Fax | |
| E-mail | finaid@valpo.edu |
| Notes | All students are encouraged to complete a free application for Federal Student Aid (FAFSA). Deadline is March 1. |

| | |
|---|---|
| Type | Vocational |
| Major | Industrial Engineering Technology |
| Scholarship Name | Charles Award |
| City | Hammond |
| Organization | Purdue University Calumet |
| Amount | Contact Financial Aid Office |
| Annual/One-Time | One Time |
| Requirements | Awarded to applicants from middle-income families. |
| Deadline | March 1 |
| Contact Name | Office of Financial Aid |
| Address | Purdue University Calumet 2200 169th Street |
| State | IN |
| Zip Code | 46323-2094 |
| Phone | 219-989-2301 |
| Fax | 219-989-2771 |
| E-mail | finaid@calumet.purdue.edu |
| Notes | Student should also complete the Purdue Calumet Merit Scholarship Application. |

| | |
|---|---|
| Type | Vocational |
| Major | Journalism |
| Scholarship Name | Tri-Kappa Journalism Scholarship |
| City | Schererville |
| Organization | Tri-Kappa Key Scholarship Committee |
| Amount | $1000 |
| Annual/One-Time | One Time |
| Requirements | This scholarship is given to a Crown Point student who is a junior in college. Applicant must be recommended by the Dean/Chairman of Journalism. |
| Deadline | January |
| Contact Name | Jennifer Sobek, Scholarship Committee |
| Address | Tri-Kappa Key Scholarship |
| State | IN |
| Zip Code | 46375 |
| Phone | 219-738-1817 |
| Fax | |
| E-mail | |
| Notes | |

| | |
|---|---|
| Type | Vocational |
| Major | Law |
| Scholarship Name | Peters, Glen D. Trust |
| City | Hammond |
| Organization | Glen D. Peters Trust |
| Amount | Open |
| Annual/One-Time | One Time |
| Requirements | Applicants must be enrolled in a school of law and a resident of Indiana. Contact through letter. |
| Deadline | Open |
| Contact Name | Cletus F. Epple, Exec. VP Glen D Peters Trust |
| Address | c/o Bank Calumet 5231 Hohman Avenue |
| State | IN |
| Zip Code | 46320 |
| Phone | 219-932-6900 |
| Fax | |
| E-mail | |
| Notes | |

| | |
|---|---|
| Type | Vocational |
| Major | Management |
| Scholarship Name | Gallagher, Albert & Margaret Business Talent Award |
| City | Hammond |
| Organization | Purdue University Calumet |
| Amount | See Financial Aid Director |
| Annual/One-Time | One Time |
| Requirements | Student must be a 2nd semester Freshman or above with a GPA of 2.0 or above. |
| Deadline | March 1 |
| Contact Name | Office of Financial Aid |
| Address | Purdue University Calumet 2200 169th Street |
| State | IN |
| Zip Code | 46323-2094 |
| Phone | 219-989-2301 |
| Fax | 219-989-2771 |
| E-mail | finaid@calumet.purdue.edu |
| Notes | |

| | |
|---|---|
| Type | Vocational |
| Major | Management |
| Scholarship Name | Management Scholarship |
| City | Hammond |
| Organization | Purdue University Calumet |
| Amount | Contact Financial Aid Office |
| Annual/One-Time | One Time |
| Requirements | Undergraduate with a combined SAT score of 1000, GPA of 3.25 and will carry 6 hours of credits. |
| Deadline | March 1 |
| Contact Name | Department of Management Scholarship |
| Address | Purdue University Calumet 2200 169th Street |
| State | IN |
| Zip Code | 46323-2094 |
| Phone | 219-989-2301 |
| Fax | 219-989-2771 |
| E-mail | finaid@calumet.purdue.edu |
| Notes | |

| | |
|---|---|
| Type | Vocational |
| Major | Mathematical Sciences |
| Scholarship Name | Clark, Donald Memorial Scholarship |
| City | Hammond |
| Organization | Purdue University Calumet |
| Amount | Contact Director of Financial Aid |
| Annual/One-Time | One Time |
| Requirements | The student must be in the top 10% of his or her class, have a GPA of 3.0 and a Math SAT score of 650. |
| Deadline | March 1 |
| Contact Name | Office of Financial Aid |
| Address | Purdue University Calumet 2200 169th Street |
| State | IN |
| Zip Code | 46323-2094 |
| Phone | 219-989-2301 |
| Fax | 219-989-2771 |
| E-mail | finaid@calumet.purdue.edu |
| Notes | Student should also complete the Purdue Calumet Merit Scholarship Application. |

| | |
|---|---|
| Type | Vocational |
| Major | Mechanical Engineering |
| Scholarship Name | Mechanical Engineering Scholarship |
| City | Valparaiso |
| Organization | Valparaiso University |
| Amount | $2000 |
| Annual/One-Time | One Time |
| Requirements | A full-time junior or senior undergraduate. Must have a minimum of a 3.8 GPA. |
| Deadline | April |
| Contact Name | Director of Financial Aid |
| Address | Valparaiso University Kretzmann Hall |
| State | IN |
| Zip Code | 46383 |
| Phone | 219-464-5015 or |
| Fax | |
| E-mail | finaid@valpo.edu |
| Notes | All students are encouraged to complete a free application for Federal Student Aid (FAFSA). Deadline is March 1. |

| | |
|---|---|
| Type | Vocational |
| Major | Medicine |
| Scholarship Name | Binkler, Dr E.B. Medical Scholarship Fund |
| City | Indianapolis |
| Organization | Indiana University |
| Amount | See Financial Aid Office |
| Annual/One-Time | One Time |
| Requirements | Must be a student in the School of Medicine at Indiana University. |
| Deadline | Contact Scholarship Fund |
| Contact Name | Dr. E.B. Binkler Medical Scholarship Fund |
| Address | c/o Financial Aid Office Indiana University Medical Center |
| State | IN |
| Zip Code | 46223 |
| Phone | |
| Fax | |
| E-mail | |
| Notes | All students are encouraged to complete a free application for Federal Student Aid (FAFSA). Deadline is March 1. |

| | |
|---|---|
| Type | Vocational |
| Major | Nursing |
| Scholarship Name | Community Colleges of Indiana Nursing Scholarship (Ivy Tech) |
| City | Gary |
| Organization | Community College of Indiana |
| Amount | See Director of Financial Aid |
| Annual/One-Time | One Time |
| Requirements | A student enrolled in the nursing program may apply. The student must attend either full-time (12 credit hours or more) or part-time (6-11 credit hours), maintain a 2.0 GPA and demonstrate financial need. Applicants must also agree to work as a nurse in an Indiana health care setting for at least two (2) years following graduation. |
| Deadline | See Director of Financial Aid |
| Contact Name | Director of Financial Aid |
| Address | Community Colleges of Indiana 1440 E. 35th Ave. |
| State | IN |
| Zip Code | 46409 |
| Phone | 219-980-1111 |
| Fax | |
| E-mail | |
| Notes | All students are encouraged to complete a free application for Federal Student Aid (FAFSA). Deadline is March 1. |

| | |
|---|---|
| Type | Vocational |
| Major | Nursing |
| Scholarship Name | Ellis, Joyce Dr. Associate Nursing Scholarship |
| City | Hammond |
| Organization | Purdue University Calumet |
| Amount | Contact Director of Financial Aid |
| Annual/One-Time | One Time |
| Requirements | Student must be a Freshman or Sophomore in the top 10% and a GPA of 3.0. Must working towards an Associate Nursing Degree and be enrolled for 12 or more hours. |
| Deadline | March 1 |
| Contact Name | Office of Financial Aid |
| Address | Purdue University of Calumet 2200 169th Street |
| State | IN |
| Zip Code | 46323-2094 |
| Phone | 219-989-2301 |
| Fax | 219-989-2771 |
| E-mail | finaid@calumet.purdue.edu |
| Notes | All students are encouraged to complete a free application for Federal Student Aid (FAFSA) and Merit Scholarship Application. |

| | |
|---|---|
| Type | Vocational |
| Major | Nursing |
| Scholarship Name | Ellis, Joyce Dr. Baccalaureate Nursing Award |
| City | Hammond |
| Organization | Purdue University Calumet |
| Amount | Contact Office of Financial Aid |
| Annual/One-Time | One Time |
| Requirements | Must be a junior or senior student in the baccalaureate nursing program, have a 3.5 GPA, and enrolled for 6 hours. |
| Deadline | March 1 |
| Contact Name | Office of Financial Aid |
| Address | Purdue University Calumet 2200 169th Street |
| State | IN |
| Zip Code | 46323-2094 |
| Phone | 219-989-2301 |
| Fax | 219-989-2771 |
| E-mail | finaid@calumet.purdue.edu |
| Notes | Merit Scholarship Application required. |

| | |
|---|---|
| Type | Vocational |
| Major | Nursing |
| Scholarship Name | Ellis, Joyce Dr. Merit Scholarship |
| City | Hammond |
| Organization | Purdue University Calumet |
| Amount | Contact Director of Financial Aid |
| Annual/One-Time | One Time |
| Requirements | Must be in the top 10% of the class with a GPA of 3.0 and enrolled in 12 hours. |
| Deadline | March 1 |
| Contact Name | Office of Financial Aid |
| Address | Purdue University Calumet 2200 169th Street |
| State | IN |
| Zip Code | 46323-2094 |
| Phone | 219-989-2301 |
| Fax | 219-989-2771 |
| E-mail | finaid@calumet.purdue.edu |
| Notes | Merit Scholarship Application required. |

| | |
|---|---|
| Type | Vocational |
| Major | Nursing |
| Scholarship Name | Powers, Donald S. Nursing Scholarship |
| City | Hammond |
| Organization | Purdue University Calumet |
| Amount | Contact Director of Financial Aid |
| Annual/One-Time | One Time |
| Requirements | Recipient should be seeking an Associate Degree in Nursing. |
| Deadline | March 1 |
| Contact Name | Office of Financial Aid |
| Address | Purdue University Calumet 2200 169th Street |
| State | IN |
| Zip Code | 46323-2094 |
| Phone | 219-989-2301 |
| Fax | 219-989-2771 |
| E-mail | finaid@calumet.purdue.edu |
| Notes | All students are encouraged to complete a free application for Federal Student Aid (FAFSA). Deadline is March 1. |

| | |
|---|---|
| Type | Vocational |
| Major | Nursing or Business |
| Scholarship Name | Crump, Thomas Friends of |
| City | Gary |
| Organization | Gary Educational Development Foundation |
| Amount | $2000—$4000 |
| Annual/One-Time | Annual |
| Requirements | The student must be graduating from Roosevelt High School in Gary, have a record of positive school experiences and achievement, has a GPA of "C" of better, has a good record of service to the school, community and church and displays positive qualities as observed directly or through references. |
| Deadline | April |
| Contact Name | High School Guidance Counselor or |
| Address | The Gary Educational Development Foundation 3757 W. 21st Ave. |
| State | IN |
| Zip Code | 46404 |
| Phone | 219 977-2192 |
| Fax | 219-977-6258 |
| E-mail | |
| Notes | |

| | |
|---|---|
| Type | Vocational |
| Major | Nursing, dietetics, industrial arts |
| Scholarship Name | Peeples, Marion D. & Eva S. Foundation |
| City | Indianapolis |
| Organization | Marion D. & Eva Peeples Foundation |
| Amount | $1000—$3000 |
| Annual/One-Time | One Time |
| Requirements | A graduating senior pursuing studies in the required major's at an Indiana school. Must provide autobiography, references, financial need analysis. Send self-addressed stamped envelope. |
| Deadline | March |
| Contact Name | Marion D. & Eva Peeples Foundation |
| Address | c/o Banc One, Indianapolis NA 111 Monument Circle |
| State | IN |
| Zip Code | 46277-0115 |
| Phone | 317-321-8189 |
| Fax | 317-321-8588 |
| E-mail | |
| Notes | |

| | |
|---|---|
| Type | Vocational |
| Major | Restaurant, Hotel and Institutional Mgmt. |
| Scholarship Name | RHI Talent Award |
| City | Hammond |
| Organization | Purdue University Calumet |
| Amount | Contact Financial Aid Office |
| Annual/One-Time | One Time |
| Requirements | For an undergraduate student in RHI with a GPA 2.0 and enrolled in 12 credit hours. |
| Deadline | March |
| Contact Name | Office of Financial Aid |
| Address | Purdue University Calumet 2200 169th Street |
| State | IN |
| Zip Code | 46323-2094 |
| Phone | 219-989-2301 |
| Fax | 219-989-2771 |
| E-mail | finaid@calumet.purdue.edu |
| Notes | Students need to complete a Merit Scholarship Application |

| | |
|---|---|
| Type | Vocational |
| Major | Restaurant, Hotel and Institutional Mgt. |
| Scholarship Name | Chicago Food Brokers Association |
| City | Hammond |
| Organization | Purdue University Calumet |
| Amount | Contact Financial Aid Office |
| Annual/One-Time | One Time |
| Requirements | Student must have a GPA of 3.0 and have an interest in pursuing a career in a food-related industry. |
| Deadline | March 1 |
| Contact Name | Office of Financial Aid |
| Address | Purdue University Calumet 2200 169th Street |
| State | IN |
| Zip Code | 46323-2094 |
| Phone | 219-989-2301 |
| Fax | 219-989-2771 |
| E-mail | finaid@calumet.purdue.edu |
| Notes | Student should also complete the Purdue Calumet Merit Scholarship Application. |

| | |
|---|---|
| Type | Vocational |
| Major | Special Education |
| Scholarship Name | Porter, Rutherford B. Scholarship |
| City | Connersville |
| Organization | Rutherford Porter Scholarship |
| Amount | $1200 |
| Annual/One-Time | One Time |
| Requirements | Applicant must demonstrate a sincere desire to participate and develop activities which contribute locally to persons in need. This award is for juniors, seniors and above who are enrolled in 12 credit hours. |
| Deadline | May |
| Contact Name | Pamela J. Musick |
| Address | East Central Special Services 3440 E. County Rd., 250 N. |
| State | IN |
| Zip Code | 47331 |
| Phone | |
| Fax | |
| E-mail | |
| Notes | Student must complete the Rutherford B. Porter Scholarship Application. |

# Links to Financial Aid and Scholarship Websites

*www.Scholarships.com*—Link to 60,000 scholarships awards
*www.Scholarships.Kachinatech.com*—Link to minority awards
*www.hsf.net* —Hispanic scholarship awards
*www.gmsp.org*—Gates Millennium Scholarship Program
*www.finaid.org*—Database search
*www.CollegeNet.com*—College and loan info with links to other high profile sites and financial aid offices of the Ivy League and Seven Sisters Schools, Inc.
*www.lib.msu.edu*—Provides information about scholarships from around the country, provides books and other valuable information.

**Send Orders To**
*iuniverse.com*
Or
*Klissell@yahoo.com*
**Postal Orders (check or money orders only)**
**3 Point Communications**
**8044 Lakewood Avenue**
**Gary, IN 46403**
(Allow 4—6 weeks for delivery)

Name_____

Company Name_____

Address_____

City_____State_____Zip_____

Please send____copies of *The Northwest Indiana Directory of Local Scholarships 2001—2002* @ _____ each*

**Sales Tax**
Add 5% for books shipped to Indiana addresses. Non-profits and Indiana organizations must include Tax-exempt or Federal ID#, otherwise you will be charged Indiana sales tax.

**Shipping**
Add $2.00 for the first book and $1.00 for each additional book

Total Enclosed: (Book(s)+Tax+Shipping) $_____

# Interested In Listing Your Scholarship? Fill Out The Form:

## SCHOLARSHIP INFORMATION FORM

Please complete thoroughly (PRINT OR TYPE)

Name of Scholarship:_____
_____

Name of Organization Presenting Scholarship:_____
_____

Requirements (Please be specific):
*Total amount:_____ Number awarded_____*

*Awarded (yearly, quarterly etc…):_____*

*Academic, financial need, other requirements:_____*

Major(s):_____
_____

Deadline:_____
_____

Contact Name(s):_____
_____

Address:_____
_____

City:_____ State_____ Zip_____

Phone:_____ Fax:_____ email:_____

*Klissell@yahoo.com* or 3 Point Communications 8044 Lakewood Avenue Gary, IN 46403

# REFERENCES

Access LaPorte County (www.lc-link.org)
Calumet College of St. Joseph
Gary Educational Development Foundation
Indiana University Northwest
Ivy Tech State College
Lake County Public Library
Purdue University Calumet
Purdue University North Central
Unity Foundation
Valparaiso University